What Really Happens In Therapy

Behind Closed Doors: A Guided Journey to Healing

Stacy G. Nation, LCSW, BCD

GO BE YOU

ISBN 919 8 218 52002 1

eISBN 979 8 996 1176 1 1

This book is dedicated to YOU, the reader.
Picking up a book like this.
Filling in the pages.
Reflecting on your life.
That all takes courage.
Thank you for being brave.
Go Be You!

ACKNOWLEDGEMENTS

In my lifetime, I have read hundreds of books, and I always read the acknowledgments because each author had a village of people helping them reach the finish line. The same is true for me. Here's my village.

This book would not have happened without the people behind the scenes helping me with the logistics. Thank you to Adam Renvoize for the cover design and Lanette Sweeney for the copy editing and proofreading. I started off having no idea how to get this into the world, and you both were very patient with me. Thank you.

To every client who has walked across the threshold of my office or logged into my Zoom room—you are the true gifts. You have taught me about attunement, trust, and what a therapeutic relationship actually is. You remind me that this journey is a human one. While I hold space for you, you are teaching me through your courage, your bravery, your willingness to be vulnerable, and your healing. Thank you for the privilege of including me on your journey.

I am grateful to have so many colleagues who have influenced my clinical and professional journey. This work is not done alone, and I have been lucky enough to have people who have been in the trenches with me—taking calls, answering texts, and talking through the hard things. Shoutout to Kate, Jen, Jon, Joe, and Meagan. Never underestimate the power of your impact. I love you all.

To Bryan Post—thank you for taking a risk on me. When

our paths crossed, I was on my own journey of parenting and breaking generational cycles. You literally held me in those big feelings that had to come out of my body. And then, over the last two decades, you have held space for some major events in my life, always reminding me that it will be okay, that I will be okay, that I am exactly where I should be. Thank you for writing the foreword to this book and for changing the lives of so many of us.

To every Soldier I have served with—I had no idea that I was entering the Army to work through the generational trauma of my family. Each of you holds a special place in my heart. I am forever grateful for the stories you have shared with me, the laughter we have had, the tears we have cried, and the adventures we have traveled together. To my Vice Bloc crew—there are no words for how much you three have helped me through some wild times. Thank you for all of the corrective experiences I needed and for reminding me that men can be safe.

To my friends who have loved me through various seasons of good and hard—Meg, Megan, Christina, Morgan, Lenaya, Kjersten, Cecelia, Hannah, Deb, and Lexi. You each see a different part of me and hold space through the celebrations and the heavy times.

Kaydi—you have been with me since I started having these big dreams. You have held my hand, answered the phone, talked me off the ledge, reminded me that visions also need executable plans, and loved me through all of my ugly seasons. Thank you will never be enough. You are my ride or die. I am grateful every day for our kindred connection.

Mom—I am so grateful that you are my mother. The journey of the mother-daughter relationship is beautiful and painful. You have held so many big feelings for me and you have shaped who I am. You are my biggest cheerleader, and you have taught me what it means to truly show up, even when you cannot fix things. Thank you for loving me and never giving up on me.

To my true inspiration for healing—my children Stella and Sage. I am in awe of both of you and your own journey. You have taught me all about unconditional love, co-regulation, healing, and the power of repair. I will forever be rooting for you. I love you to the moon and back, through the stars, and around the sun.

To Odin Michael and Titan George—two puppers who allowed me to engage in patterned, repetitive, bilateral activity when I needed emotional regulation most. Good boys.

And this book would never have come to fruition without my husband. Billy, thank you. For becoming my safe space. For doing your own work. For loving me when I am unlovable. For choosing to be with a woman who has suitcases of baggage. For sorting out the baggage with me. For dreaming big with me and then chasing those dreams. Mostly, thank you for coming to a Red Rocks concert and allowing this whole journey to begin.

I love you, B Cal.

Contents

Disclaimer

This book is intended for educational and informational purposes only. It is not a substitute for professional mental-health treatment, medical advice, or clinical care. The information, tools, and frameworks presented in these pages are designed to support self-awareness and personal growth—they do not constitute therapy and do not establish a therapeutic relationship between the author and the reader.

If you are experiencing a mental-health crisis, thoughts of suicide or self-harm, or any other urgent concern, please contact a qualified mental health professional immediately or call or text 988, *the Suicide and Crisis Lifeline, available 24 hours a day. Veterans and active-duty service members can also reach the Veterans Crisis Line at* 988, *then press* 1.

The author is a Licensed Clinical Social Worker (LCSW) *and Board Certified Diplomate* (BCD). *Nothing in this book should be interpreted as clinical advice specific to your individual situation.*

A Note on Stories

The client stories in this book are composites drawn from more than 20 *years of clinical practice. Details, including names, identifying characteristics, and circumstances, have been changed to protect confidentiality. Any resemblance to specific individuals is coincidental. All named individuals outside of clinical contexts are real people who have given their permission to be included.*

Every story, clinical framework, and insight in these pages is the author's own. The words themselves came from over 20 years of sitting across from people who trusted this author with their hardest moments.

Permissions and Credits

For permissions, bulk orders, speaking inquiries, or course information, visit https://www.gobeyou.org.

FOREWORD

There are very few people in this field who are willing to tell the truth about what really happens in therapy.

Stacy Nation is one of them.

I have known Stacy for nearly 20 years, and in that time I have watched her do something that most clinicians never quite find the courage to do, she has been willing to evolve. Not just professionally, but personally. She has allowed her work to be shaped not by theory alone, but by sitting across from real people in real pain, over and over again, and asking a better question.

Not what is wrong with you.

But what happened to you.

That shift changes everything.

In a world where mental health is often reduced to diagnoses, labels, and symptom management, Stacy brings us back to something far more honest, and far more useful, the human nervous system, and the stories it carries. This book is not built on abstract ideas or recycled clinical language. It is built on more than 20,000 conversations with people who trusted her with their hardest moments, and on a willingness to look at what actually works when the door is closed and it is just a therapist and a human being trying to make sense of pain.

That is what makes this book different.

Stacy does not hide behind the safety of traditional frameworks when they fall short. She names, clearly and directly, that talk alone is not enough, that insight without integration leaves people stuck, and that healing requires working with the body, not just the mind. These are not easy statements to make in a field that has been built on talking, analyzing, and repeating. But they are necessary.

And Stacy is bold enough to say them.

What I have always respected about Stacy is not just her clinical skill, though she has that in abundance. It is her presence. Her willingness to sit in the discomfort with people. To not rush them out of it. To not fix, rescue, or control. But to guide. To teach. To help people understand that their responses make sense, that their nervous system has been doing its job, and that there is a way forward that does not require shame.

You will feel that as you read this book.

You will also feel her honesty. Stacy does not position herself above the work. She places herself inside of it. She shares her own story, her own learning, her own moments of getting it wrong, and that matters. Because the best clinicians are not the ones who have mastered theory, they are the ones who have done their own work.

Stacy has done that work.

Her experience spans private practice, work with families, and service with the military, which means she has sat with a wide range of human experience, from everyday stress to profound trauma. And across all of those environments, she has stayed anchored in one core truth, healing does not come from fear. It comes from understanding, safety, and the ability to complete what the nervous system has been trying to finish.

That is the heart of this book.

What you will find in these pages is not a quick fix. It is not surface-level advice. It is a framework that will ask you to look at yourself differently. To move from judgment to curiosity. To begin understanding your reactions not as flaws, but as patterns that were built for a reason.

And once you see that, you cannot unsee it.

That is both the challenge and the gift of this work.

I have had the honor of mentoring Stacy over the years, and one of the greatest privileges in that relationship has been watching her step fully into her own voice. She is passionate. She is bold. And she is deeply committed to helping people suffer less, not someday, but now.

This book is an extension of that commitment.

If you are willing to be honest with yourself, if you are willing to move beyond what you have been told about healing, and if you are ready to understand what is actually happening inside of you, this book will meet you there.

And it will change you.

Bryan Post

Brock, Texas

A NOTE BEFORE YOU BEGIN

This book is rooted in over 20 years of clinical practice and more than 20,000 one-on-one conversations. It is written by a therapist, informed by therapy, and designed to give you access to the tools and frameworks that make therapy work.

But this book is not therapy.

What this book cannot do is be a witness to your story. Finding an attuned clinician who can witness, mirror, and hold space for you can be priceless—offering a safe, contained relationship in which corrective experiences become possible in ways no book can replicate. If you have access to that kind of support, I encourage you to seek it. If you are already in therapy, this book is designed to deepen and support that work, not replace it.

That said, the barriers to accessing a real, live, well-matched therapist are real. Cost. Insurance. Vulnerability. The courage it takes to open up to a stranger. It sometimes takes six or seven attempts to find the right fit. Those barriers are exactly why this book needs to exist—to put effective, evidence-informed tools into the hands of people who need them, wherever they are, whatever their circumstances.

This book will teach you. It will guide you. It will walk beside you through some difficult and important territory. What it cannot do is see you the way another human being can.

If at any point the material in these pages surfaces something that feels beyond what a book can hold, please reach out for professional support. In the United States, the 988 Suicide and Crisis Lifeline is available by call or text, 24 hours a day. For the Veterans' Crisis Line: Dial 988 then Press 1, or chat online at veteranscrisisline.net, or text 838255.

INTRODUCTION

Everything You're Afraid to Look at Has Already Happened

Everything you're afraid to look at has already happened—and you lived through it.

Every hard thing, every moment you are trying to avoid, every moment you do not want to think about, every situation that causes your body to go into full-alert mode—you've already survived all of that. This complex dance that your brain, mind, and body does is why you've picked up this book. At a very conscious level, your mind knows that the "thing" has already happened. But the rest of you...your body, parts of your brain, your nervous system in its entirety—they haven't gotten the message yet. And that gap—between what happened and what your nervous system is still carrying—is exactly what this book is about.

I've spent over 20 years as a licensed clinical social worker, sitting across from people in a therapy room: I've worked with Soldiers, parents, 20-somethings trying to break patterns they didn't choose, mothers triggered by their own mothers, men who love their kids and can't understand why their kids' tantrums send them somewhere dark and distant, Veterans who can't sleep, and people who know—they *know*—that their emotional reactions are bigger than the moment in front of them but just don't know why.

Over the course of more than 20,000 one-on-one conversations, I kept seeing the same thing: People getting stuck. They weren't stuck because they weren't trying, nor because they weren't brave enough or committed enough. But the tools they'd been given—talk, analyze, revisit, repeat—weren't closing a stress cycle, a loop that has been continuously activated.

A quick note about stress cycles. When our body and brain experience something stressful, we get activated. In order to come back to a place of homeostasis, we must allow our entire being to move through that stress, also known as closing the stress cycle. Talk therapy alone doesn't close the stress cycle. We will go further into this in Chapter 2.

I also kept meeting people who couldn't access therapy at all. The cost was too high. The insurance wasn't there. There was not a therapist in the region who specialized in or understood the topic: Veterans, marital issues, personality disorders, adoption, reactive attachment, childhood trauma, etc. Or some people simply couldn't imagine opening up to a stranger about the things they'd worked so hard to hold in and hold together. I understood that. And I thought—what if I could give people tools they could use in the privacy of their own homes? Tools based on neuroscience, not guesswork. Tools that actually get us where we need to go.

That's this book.

I want you to know something about the therapists who are good at this work, at being therapists—the ones who have actually been in therapy themselves, explored their own stressors, and addressed their traumatic events. We therapists are rooting for you. We do not want you to suffer one day longer than you have to. And we know that your brain is built to protect you. Even as you read this book, even as you try these skills, **your brain will not take you somewhere you are not ready to go.** You are safer in this process than you think.

Here's something else most people don't know about how therapy is meant to work. Therapists don't want to see you every week for 20 years. What we want is to be your therapist over a lifetime. You come in, you work on the stressful moment or season, you close the stress cycles for that stage of life, and then you go live. You return when the next stage brings something that needs to be closed. That's it. This book is built on that same idea. You are not broken and do not need endless fixing. You are a human being moving through life, and sometimes you get caught in a loop that needs to be closed.

When you first start closing cycles, the work may feel heavy and hard. That's because you are addressing a lifetime of cycles. Once you get through that initial hard stage, therapy should be maintenance in which you take care of your brain and body and release the stress of the current season. It will not always be as hard, or at least it should not always be.

This book is for you if you are tired of suffering. If you feel like your reactions to life are stronger than the events that are causing them. If you're ready to stop just surviving and start understanding why your nervous system does what it does—and what to do about it.

You don't have to feel this way forever.

This book is also for you if you know that you did not grow up with templates or models for how to manage stress, trauma, and conflict. Many of us grew up in homes where we learned early on how to make everyone else comfortable—at the expense of our own health. This book is for you.

That's the promise of this book. Not a quick fix. Not a magical cure. But real tools, grounded in science, that will help you understand yourself, complete the cycles your nervous system is still holding, and step into your life with more clarity and more presence than you have right now.

Every chapter will have a journaling space that allows you to answer questions from your own life about the content of that chapter. You can come back to these at any time. If you'd rather type your answers, you can download the journaling prompts in a complete guided workbook at this QR code.

Slow is fast here. Take your time. Listen to your body. Set this book down when you need to and pick it back up when you're ready. Let's begin.

PART ONE

The Foundation

Your brain is doing exactly what it was built to do.

CHAPTER ONE

Meet Your Brain

The Story

Corey was eight years old, and we were always quietly relieved when he didn't show up for school.

I'm not proud of that. But it's the truth. And, I want to share truths with you, even the hard ones, the ones that people judge us for. You may have your own truths that live within you.

Corey's real name isn't mine to share, but his story is—because it changed everything for me. He would arrive already dysregulated, his nervous system wound so tight that by mid-morning, he was knocking computers off desks, sending chairs airborne, and causing the adults around him to brace for any other major behaviors that might happen next. On the worst days, we spent six to eight hours physically restraining this child to get him through a single school day. Six to eight hours restraining an eight-year-old boy. And a team of adults, myself included, genuinely believed we were helping him.

Then, came the day I will remember forever. A day that has defined my professional work.

Three of us had just come out of a restraint - Corey, myself, and my teammate. We had been through this so many times before. Coming out of a restraint means everyone appears emotionally regulated - or at least that's what we told ourselves. We were all regulated enough to re-enter the world. We were leaving the seclusion room and he turned towards me and gave me the hardest titty twister of my life. He grabbed my breast and twisted, refusing to let go. Thankfully, my reaction was a flight response, not fight response.

I grabbed his hands and said firmly, "Don't ever do that again." I left the situation, painful boob intact, and went to our office to call his mom. I told her what happened. I felt the overwhelming shame that comes from knowing that what I thought was the right answer was actually the very wrong answer.

It wasn't until a year later—after a conference that shifted the entire way of thinking about children, stress, and how we approach them— that the full irony of that moment landed.

We had been putting our hands on that child for months. Restraining him. Holding him down. And we were shocked—genuinely shocked—when he put his hands on us.

This situation was at the beginning of my career, over 20 years ago. This was during a time when restraints and seclusion were used more frequently. The science does not support what we were doing and never did. We called our restraints intervention, but his nervous system experienced what we did as a threat. And you cannot heal a threat response by threatening someone further. I know that now. I wish I had known it then. There are a thousand things I would do differently. But I didn't know what I didn't know—until the day I walked into a conference looking only for continuing education credits.

The Science

I was sitting in the middle row, right side, when Dr. Bruce Perry started speaking. He was the keynote speaker. I had never heard of him or any of his work.

I don't remember deciding to go quiet; it just happened.

The room kept moving around me—people taking notes, shifting in their seats—but I sat completely still. Not because I was bored but because something inside me was reorganizing.

Dr. Bruce Perry has spent decades helping people understand how the brain develops, how trauma impacts brain development through what he calls the Neurosequential Model, and what we can do to assist in the healing of the trauma that happens during development.

I want to pause here for a moment to recognize the brain's complexity. The model I use to describe brain development in this book is a clinical simplification. Neuroscience has evolved significantly, and the brain is far more integrated and complex than older models suggest. What remains true —and what this book is built on —is the clinical observation that, under stress and activation, our survival responses come online faster than our reasoning does—and that healing requires working with the body and the nervous system, not just the thinking mind. I use simplified language because it is useful, not because it is the complete picture.

In the therapy room, we use simplified clinical frameworks because those are helpful to people who are healing. The following information is exactly what I would tell you if you were sitting on the couch across from me in my office.

What follows is my simplified version of Dr. Perry's Neurosequential Model framework—broken down to be intentionally accessible, not exhaustive. For the complete science, Perry's work is essential reading and you'll find references to it in the resources at the back of this book. But here is what over 20 years of applying these concepts taught me about what his research means for your life.

That day Dr. Perry was explaining how the brain develops and how it builds from the bottom up. While the entire brain is fully present when we are born, we know that neuropathways are busy being created during different stages of development.

Dr. Perry explained how the earliest experiences of a child's life wire the nervous system in ways that shape everything that comes after—behavior, relationships, the ability to feel safe, and the ability to learn. If a child is born into a safe, loving, emotionally regulated environment, the nervous system is wired in safety. If a child is born in a setting where there is intense emotion, high conflict, loss of attachment, or addiction, the child's nervous system is wired for protection, activating the stress response of fight, flight or freeze.

He was explaining in plain language what was actually happening with Corey, telling me why restraint would never work and why what looked like defiance and aggression was actually survival.

Dr. Perry explained bottom-up strategies. The concept that when we regulate the bottom of the brain (the brainstem or survival center) before we try to regulate the top of the brain (the cortex or reasoning center) we will regulate a child more effectively, creating safety first. This made sense to me. When we try to talk someone out of their feelings, or talk them down from a big emotion, the other person often gets more frustrated. Instead, if we go for a walk, move our bodies, have a snack, give a hug, or actively listen with less words, the person will become emotionally regulated sooner.

In the situation with Corey, he was arriving at school with a stress response system already activated, scanning for threat. His nervous system told him that school, or the people within the school, was dangerous and he should do all that he can to get out of that situation. Instead of co-regulating him and offering strategies for regulation, we were maintaining his activation and ending up in a restraint, which further supported the messaging of his brain, "This system is threatening, do what you can to get out of it." Corey's response was a fight response and showed up in aggressive and violent behaviors.

I thought about what Corey's face looked like when he was

dysregulated. I thought about the relief we felt when he was absent. And I felt all of the feelings (shame, embarrassment, sadness, despair) of someone who has been doing harm while trying to do good.

Later, when I began speaking to my own audiences about this science, I noticed something familiar. A silence fell over the crowd. A stillness. People sitting quietly, focused. I used to think I was losing them. I've come to understand that's what it looks like when a person's worldview internally recognizes new information that is life-changing.

That's what we're going to do in this chapter. We're going to meet your brain—not to overwhelm you with science, but to give you the same roadmap that changed everything for me.

Here's what you need to know. (Remember that there are so many ways to talk about the brain. This is the most helpful for the clients that I see.)

Your brain develops from the bottom up and the inside out. The brainstem develops first—in utero through about nine months old. This is your survival center. It houses your sensory system and your fight, flight, and freeze responses. Science shares that there are other responses as well, but to keep this simple, we are sticking with fight, flight, and freeze. This part of your brain doesn't think. It reacts based on all of the information, internally and externally that it is taking in through the brain. The brain processes this information in milliseconds. It doesn't reason. Its only job is to keep you alive—to protect you.

I spend the most time talking with my clients about this part of the brain. This is why a Veteran can hear an alarm in Walmart and hit the ground, reacting as if there's an incoming bomb. Or, this is why a child can smell coffee breath on a teacher and react with aggression because her abuser had coffee breath. There is not reasoning, just protecting.

Next in brain development comes the midbrain, which further develops between ages four and six and supports emotional regulation. Then the limbic system, develops throughout childhood and adolescence, and supports social connection and relationships. And finally the cortex—the thinking, reflecting, decision-making part of your brain—which doesn't fully develop until your mid-twenties. I often say that the cortex is an adult's worst enemy because we have a fully developed cortex and the children in our lives do not! We try to reason with kids and they do not have enough neuropathways developed to reason like we do.

Again, you have a whole brain at birth, and complex neural systems develop throughout our lifetime, giving us various stages of development.

This matters for one reason above all others. When stress or trauma occurs before the brain is fully developed—or when your nervous system is already highly activated—you cannot think your way out of it. You cannot talk yourself into calm. You cannot reason with a brainstem.

Corey wasn't choosing his behavior. He was surviving it.

And if you've ever wondered why you react the way you do—if you've ever felt like your responses are bigger than the moment in front of you, like something takes over before you even have a chance to think—this is why. Your brain is doing exactly what it was built to do. It learned to protect you—and it got very good at its job.

The Skill: Meet Your Brain

The first skill this book will teach you isn't a breathing exercise or a journaling prompt. It's simpler than that.

It's a reframe: REFLECT ON THE JOURNEY OF YOUR OWN BRAIN DEVELOPMENT.

Instead of asking, "What is wrong with me?" I want you to begin asking, "From what was my nervous system keeping me safe?" What was happening in your own life as your brain was developing? What happened to you?

Let's talk about the nervous system. We are living in a world where this phrase is used constantly, in TikTok mental-health videos, on other social media, in a world where everything is about "calming your nervous system." That's not what this book is about. This book is about truly understanding HOW your nervous system works, how it protects you, and how you move through the complexity of that protection so that you can live a life of less activation, fewer triggers, and more presence.

In order for us to understand our brain, we must also understand what the nervous system actually is. The nervous system is a complex network of nerves and cells that carries messages to and from the brain and spinal cord out to other parts of the body. Many people think of the nervous system just as the body. However, the brain is signaling the body constantly. So throughout this book, when we discuss "your nervous system," I want you to understand I mean both the brain and the body–they are inseparable.

Back to the questions: From what was your nervous system keeping you safe? What was happening in your own life as your brain was developing?

Making that shift from judgment to curiosity is no small thing. Switching from self-blame to curiosity is, in many ways, the entire foundation of healing. You cannot work with a nervous system with which you are at war. You cannot complete a stress cycle of which you are afraid. You cannot heal what you cannot first understand with compassion.

As you read this chapter and meet your brain, I want you to hold those questions (about what you were going through when) gently. Just let these questions sit somewhere in your body and notice what happens.

From what was your nervous system keeping you safe? You can figure this out by looking at what was happening in your life as your brain was developing.

Think about your brain developing from the bottom up and what was happening to you at each developmental stage. Reflect back to your in utero experiences, your birth story, your life as an infant, toddler, early childhood. Reflect on your elementary, middle, and high school years.

Notice your body as you reflect. Notice your thoughts. Notice your feelings. Feel free to jot down what comes to mind.

From My Life

Throughout my life, I have had many opportunities to reflect on the development of my brain and which incidents in my childhood impacted that development. One story stands out.

I am the daughter of an alcoholic father and a mother who has been recovering from codependence, the oldest of three girls. I have an ACE score of seven.

A quick note here. ACE stands for Adverse Childhood Experiences. This is a survey of 10 questions asking about various adverse experiences someone had during childhood (child abuse, neglect, sexual abuse, witnessing domestic violence, etc.) While the list is not comprehensive, and we have learned so much more in the past decade about childhood experiences, an ACE score can tell a clinician a lot about what a child experienced in their nervous system.

Back to my ACE score of seven. In plain terms, this score means my nervous system was constantly activated for protection and to keep me safe.

My reflections on my own brain development began when I was 18, sitting in my Intro to Psychology class. I was in my first year of college, my first semester, when I encountered the word, "alcoholic."

I remember the feeling exactly. I was silent. Quiet. Still. I was experiencing the same internal reorganizing that happens when the brain is shifting. Here was a word—a real word, a clinical word, a word that existed in textbooks—that described what was happening inside my home. I wasn't crazy. I wasn't dramatic. There was a name for it.

But I couldn't tell anyone yet. My parents were still married. My sisters were still living at home. I was the only one who had the language, and I carried it alone for a long time before my secrets could be told.

My father would get drunk, sometimes violent, and then he would sober up with no memory of what had happened—or he would insist that what we said happened wasn't real. That's called gaslighting. I didn't have that word at 18 either. But I had the experience of it, living in my nervous system the way all experiences do, long before I had words to describe it.

As I have thought about my own brain and my own development, I have become aware of how those experiences with my father and my family of origin have shaped my entire nervous system, the way my brain functions and works, how my stress-response system was developed, and eventually what led me to become a therapist.

I became a therapist for two reasons: First because I genuinely love helping people, and second because I knew I needed to help myself. The best therapists I know have done both—they've sat in the client chair, they've done the work, and they keep doing it. In telling you what really happens in a therapy room, I hope you will see that I have been the person sitting across from the therapist, too.

This book is about helping you figure out your brain, your stressors, your healing.

Your Journey

This space is an invitation to notice—not to analyze, explain, or fix anything. You are not required to remember details or make sense of your experiences right now. This space is designed for you to write notes, doodle, draw, bullet point, or anything that allows you to put what you notice on paper.

Move slowly. Pause as needed.

1. What Stood Out

As you followed along in this chapter, notice what stood out.

This may be:

- A thought
- A feeling
- A memory
- A question
- Or something you can't quite put into words yet

You do not need to explain or interpret it.

Just note it here:

2. Developmental Moments That Came to Mind

As you learned how the brain develops from the bottom up and the inside out, were there moments in your life that surfaced?

These might relate to:

- Early childhood
- School years

- Teen years
- Early adulthood

Write down anything that came up, even if it feels small or unclear:

3. Body Awareness Check-In
Pause for a moment and notice your body right now.
Circle or write anything you're aware of:

- Calm
- Tension
- Curiosity
- Emotion
- Fatigue
- Neutral / Nothing noticeable

Where do you notice these feelings or sensations in your body?

4. Brain Development Notes

You do not need to fill this out all at once. You may return to this page at any time.

This section is not about trauma—it's about understanding context. Write down anything that you sense is relevant for these stages of development. Perhaps a sibling was born, you moved, or there was a death in the family. Perhaps you experienced a different event like abuse, neglect, or witnessed domestic violence.

Early Childhood (0–6):

School Age (7–12):

Teen Years (13–18):

Young Adulthood (18–25):

Closing Reminder

If nothing came to mind today, that's okay. If something did come up, you don't need to do anything with it yet.

If at any point this work feels overwhelming, pause, rest, engage in regulating practices, and return when you are ready.

*Regulating practices may be taking a walk, going to the gym, taking a shower, having a snack, drinking some water, listening to music, or engaging in an activity that lowers your activation and brings your body to a more regulated state.

Your brain will not take you where you are not ready to go.

CHAPTER TWO

The Stress Cycle

The Story

David, a father, came to one of my trainings because his wife asked him to.

That's how it often goes. Someone in the room has been nudged, coaxed, or lovingly dragged there by a partner who believed therapy or a training would help. The father showed up—present and willing, even if not entirely sure why he was there or what any of this had to do with him.

I've been speaking to audiences for a long time. Parents, educators, veterans, couples. And I've noticed that most people move through three stages during the workshops I lead and often during their early therapy sessions, as well.

The first stage is other-focused. They are sitting in their chair thinking about how what I'm saying applies to someone else—their student, their child, or their spouse. They are thinking, "This is helpful. I'm learning things. I can use this with the people in my life." There's a comfortable distance in this first stage. The information is interesting and useful. "I'll try these new strategies." Nothing is deeply internal yet.

The second stage is subtle and quiet. They start thinking about their own childhoods—their own stressors, their own reactivity, and their own experiences. The information becomes much more personal. The information stops being about someone else.

The third stage is the hardest. They start thinking about all the ways they believe they have gotten it wrong—with their kids, with their partners, and with themselves. This is the stage where people get very quiet, internally focused, reflecting on their own journeys.

This father moved through all three stages in about forty-five minutes.

I was talking about stress using the analogy of the rubber band. I use this analogy constantly because it's the one that lands most reliably, most viscerally, most immediately. Our nervous systems are like a rubber band. Every stressor stretches the rubber band. The more stressed we are, the more stretched we are. A regulated life allows the rubber band to stretch and release. Stretch and release.

Sometimes, we don't release. We just keep stretching. If we never give ourselves or the people we love time and the tools to release that stretch, the rubber band just keeps pulling. And pulling. Until something snaps. Some people, some children, live in this stretched-out state for months, years, decades. Some children come to us stretched from birth.

After the training, David found me. There were tears in his eyes—which I want you to notice, because fathers don't often cry in public after a Saturday morning parenting workshop. Something had landed in him in a meaningful and significant way. He said, "That rubber band analogy changed my life. I realized that every demand or request I'm making of my kid is stretching his rubber band. It keeps stretching, and I'm not helping him release any of it. So instead of play or hugs or a break—things that would release some stretch—I just add more. And we end up in this dynamic where I yell, and my kid cries. It's terrible. Now I know I need to give my child time and strategies to release their stretch (stress)."

I've thought about that moment many times since.

Not just because of what he said—but because of what it took for him to be standing there saying it. He came for his wife. He stayed for his child. And somewhere in the middle, without planning to, he found the analogy that changed his life.

A few months later, David reached out to me to tell me something remarkable. He and his child had developed a shared language. They could name what was happening in real time. And his child—a young kid—had started saying:

"This is making me stretch, Dad. I need support. I need help releasing this stretch."

A child started using those words because a father was willing to get curious in a training room on a Saturday morning and let something land.

That's what understanding the stress cycle can do. Not just for you—but for everyone in your world.

The Science

Here's what David intuitively grasped in 45 minutes that most of us were never taught at all.

Stress is not just an emotion. It's a cycle. And cycles are meant to be completed.

I want you to imagine a circle. At the top of that circle, something happens. It might be enormous—a loss, a trauma, or a crisis. Or it might be ordinary—a hard conversation, a long commute, a child's meltdown, or a comment from your mother-in-law. Big or small, your nervous system experiences it as stress.

The next part of the cycle is activation. Your fight, flight, or freeze response comes online. This is a complex part of the cycle and everyone's responses are different. In the very simplest terms, your body reacts through activation, aggression, fleeing, or shutting down. This is not a failure or a flaw. This is your nervous system doing precisely what it was built to do—preparing you to survive.

After activation, the next phase in the cycle is to come back to homeostasis. The cycle needs to be completed. The entire nervous system (brain and body) needs to move through the experience, process it, release it, and return to a baseline state. That completion is what we're wired for.

But here's what happens to most of us.

Somewhere between activation and completion, we take an off-ramp.

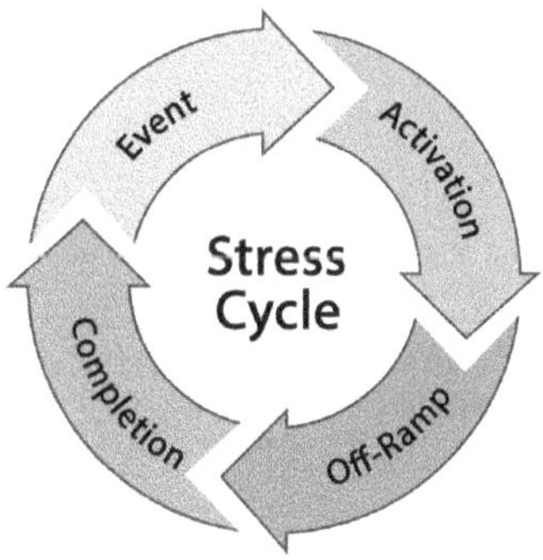

Instead of moving through the experience, and feeling it fully in our bodies, our feelings, and our thoughts, we go around it. We avoid. We distract. We shut down. We compartmentalize. We overwork. We scroll. We drink. We eat. We hit the gym. We pour another cup of coffee. We grab an energy drink or a cocktail. We stay very, very busy.

There are as many off-ramps as there are people taking them, and most of us have a preferred route we've been driving for years without realizing it's a detour. To be clear, some of these off-ramps (like going to the gym) might appear to be healthy. However, anything we do to avoid the completion of a stress cycle, to delay feeling the physiological and emotional impact of the stress that activated us, is preventing us from returning to baseline, to a state of emotional regulation.

Many of us learned our off-ramps very early. We heard messages like, "Don't cry. Be strong. Suck it up. You're fine. Stop being so sensitive." Those messages didn't usually come from cruelty. They came from people who had their own incomplete cycles and had learned their own off-ramps. We inherited the detour.

Here's what's important to understand: the off-ramp helped you. At the time, given your context, it was probably the best available option. A child who not allowed to cry (parents yell or shame the child when tears start) learns to hold in his tears because crying is not safe. A Soldier who cannot show fear learns to compartmentalize because the mission requires it. A mother who cannot fall apart learns to keep moving because people depend on her.

The nervous system is always trying to protect you. The off-ramp was your protection.

But protection has long-term impacts.

When the stress cycle is not completed, the nervous system keeps holding it. The filing cabinet of memories in your brain cannot properly file the experience. The nervous system cannot integrate the experience. The activation does not discharge. The rubber band stays stretched. And the longer it stays stretched, the less capacity it has—until even small stressors produce enormous responses, and you find yourself snapping about something that has almost nothing to do with what's actually wrong.

I've worked with clients whose bodies held incomplete stress cycles in ways that stunned their doctors. One woman's knees never healed after replacement surgery—until we traced the pain back to sexual abuse her nervous system had been holding for decades. A client had repeated seizures that had no medical explanation—until we began listening to the childhood trauma his nervous system was carrying and gave it a way to complete what it had started. The brain-body connection is powerful and protective. Every memory is stored at a cellular level.

We also need to understand that some stress cycles are dormant. We may not even know we are carrying a long-ago stressor that needs completing until something activates it. A smell, a sound, a season, a relationship dynamic—and suddenly something surfaces that had been floating around, unfiled and waiting. That's not failure. That's the nervous system revealing what it's ready to work with.

In order to complete the stress cycle, or release the rubberband, and bring our nervous systems back to homeostasis, we have to talk about emotions.

Emotions are like ocean waves. Sometimes they tickle your toes—a gentle, managcablc lapping at thc edges of your awareness. Sometimes they knock you completely off your feet, feeling like you're going to drown in the feelings. But they always recede. This is not a metaphor for the sake of poetry. This is how emotions actually function in the nervous system. Every emotion has a beginning, a peak, and an end. What extends emotions beyond their natural arc is almost always our relationship to them—the resistance, the story, the fear that if we feel this fully, the feelings and sensations will never stop. The strength of our emotions, or our feelings, is often why we take the off-ramp. We just do not want to feel something so painful, so strong.

But I'm here to tell you feeling the feelings will stop. The wave always recedes. Stress cycles are like that. As we complete them, it can feel like ocean waves, knocking us over. Once the stress cycle is completed, the feelings in our body, our heart, our mind, feel the release and return to a more emotionally regulated state, less activated.

Talk therapy alone—as valuable as it can be—often addresses thoughts and feelings while leaving the body completely out of the conversation. And the body, as you'll discover throughout this book, is where the cycle actually lives. There are three parts to every memory and every stress response: a thought, a feeling, and a body experience. Most of us are fluent in the first two. The third one is where real completion happens—and it's the piece that's almost always left out.

The Skill: Completing The Stress Cycle

The skill in this chapter is deceptively simple.

It's not a technique. It's an awareness practice. And awareness always comes before action.

I want you to start noticing your off-ramps.

Not to judge them. Not to stop them immediately. Not to white-knuckle your way past them with sheer willpower. Just to notice them. To begin building a map of your own detour routes.

You might ask yourself gently:

When stress shows up in my body, what do I do? What do I reach for? What's my body's natural reaction? What do I do instead of feeling it?

What is happening inside of me when my rubber band is stretched? What are my feelings? What are my behaviors? What are my body sensations? What am I noticing internally? And what, if anything, actually releases some of that stretch?

For some people, the off-ramp is obvious—a glass of wine at the end of every hard day, a phone that gets picked up the moment silence arrives. For others, it's subtler—a sudden urge to clean, to help someone else, to get very busy, to go completely numb. For others still, it looks healthy on the outside—the person who runs five miles every morning, not because it feels good, but because they cannot tolerate what happens if they stop moving.

There is no shame in the off-ramp. Remember—it serves as protection. We're not here to take it away before you have something better with which to replace it. We're here to see it clearly for what it is, so that eventually—slowly, safely, at your own pace—you can learn to complete the cycle instead of rerouting around it.

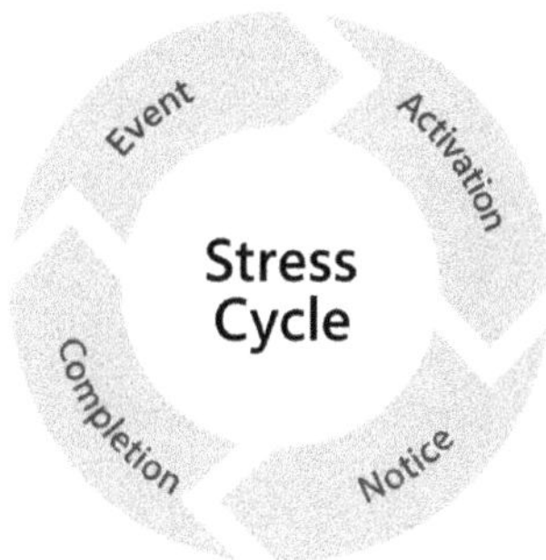

From My Life

I didn't fully understand the stress cycle in my own life until I was sitting with my Soldiers.

I'd been talking about rubber bands with many parents for years. But it wasn't until I was deployed, sitting one-on-one with young people whose nervous systems were stretched to their absolute limit, that the full picture clicked into place for me.

We spend so much time in the mental-health field—whether working with civilian or military populations—focused on the traumatic event. What happened. When it happened. How bad it was. We treat the story of the event as though the event itself is the problem to be solved.

But sitting with those Soldiers, I kept seeing the same thing. It was not just the events that were breaking them. It was the accumulation. The rubber band had been stretched for months or years with almost no release. The activation had nowhere to go. The off-ramps that worked in the short term—humor, hypervigilance, disconnection, substance use, hours in the gym, caffeine just to keep functioning—were now the only tools they had.

I started talking to them differently. Not about what happened—but about stress. About the cycle. About the off-ramps they'd been living. And something shifted in those conversations. Not because I had better questions. But because I was finally pointing at the right thing.

I also had to look at my own rubber band.

I am someone who defaults to motion when stressed. I get busy. I get productive. I help other people. For a long time, I called this a strength—and in some ways it is. But it's also one of my most reliable off-ramps. Staying in motion meant I didn't have to feel the stretch. It meant the cycle never had to be completed because there was always something else to do.

Learning to notice that—really notice it, with curiosity instead of judgment—was one of the more humbling parts of my own healing journey.

The rubber band doesn't lie. It just needs someone to finally pay attention to it.

Your Journey

As you move through this worksheet, go slowly. You are not required to complete every section in one sitting.

This work is about noticing patterns—not judging them.

1. Stressors You Notice

As you learned about the stress cycle, notice any stressors

that came to mind.

These may be:

- Big or small
- Past or recent
- Emotional, physical, or relational

You don't need to explain them.

Stressors that came up:

2. Where You Notice Activation

When a stressor happens, your nervous system responds.

As you think about the stressors you listed above, notice what activation looks like for you.

You might notice:

- Racing thoughts
- Tight chest
- Shallow breathing
- Numbness
- Urge to act or withdraw

What activation looks or feels like:

3. Off-Ramps You Learned:

Many of us learned to exit the stress cycle early in order to cope.

Some common off-ramps include:

- Shutting down
- Avoidance
- Distraction
- Food
- Alcohol
- Overworking
- Over-exercising
- Compartmentalizing

There is no shame here. These off-ramps helped you survive.

Off-ramps you recognize in yourself:

4. Messages You Received About Stress or Emotions

Often, our off-ramps are connected to messages we received growing up or in important environments.

Examples:

- "Don't cry."
- "Be strong."
- "Suck it up."
- "Move on."

Messages you remember receiving:

5. What Happens When the Cycle Isn't Completed

When stress cycles don't get completed, the nervous system continues to hold them.

As you reflect, notice anything you've experienced over time that might be connected.

This could include:

- Chronic stress
- Emotional overwhelm
- Irritability
- Fatigue

- Feeling stuck

What you've noticed over time:

6. A Gentle Reframe

This book is about learning how to complete the stress cycle—not blaming yourself for how you learned to cope.

Write one sentence to yourself that feels supportive.

Examples:

- "My body was doing its best."
- "These patterns make sense."
- "I can learn new ways now."

Your sentence:

Closing Reminder

You are not required to change anything yet. Awareness comes first.

If this part of the journey feels activating, pause and return when you are ready. Your body will move at the pace that is right for you.

CHAPTER THREE

Memory, Trauma, and the Body

The Story

I was 16 years old.

We were at hunting camp—my dad, my youngest sister, several of dad's buddies, and me. We had finished hunting for the day, and I asked if I could go have dinner with my boyfriend and his dad down the road. This was a boy I had been dating for more than a year. His dad was a man my father had gone to high school with. They had been in our lives for years. There was nothing unusual about the ask.

When I came back, my dad had clearly been drinking.

He threw me up against a trailer and put his hands around my neck. He said—and I remember every word, "You are such a slut. Where have you been, whore?"

I was scared. I was devastated. I was shocked.

I could see my youngest sister across the camp. Her eyes were wide. Her face was filled with terror. I can still see that face.

And I could see the grown men standing there. My dad's friends. Men I had known for several years, all doing nothing.

Eventually, my father took his hands off my throat. I

grabbed my keys and left. I asked my sister to come with me, but she stayed, knowing the fallout of her leaving would be worse than if she stayed.

This was not the first time my father had been violent. There had been other times—times when I was younger, more dependent, with nowhere to go and no way to leave, times when I was stuck in the way that children are stuck, too small and too reliant to do anything but survive.

This event feels the most significant, not because it was the worst thing my father ever did. It feels significant because it was the first time I had agency. For the first time I was old enough and independent enough to make a choice. I could leave. And I did.

What I didn't fully understand until much later—until I was writing this book, actually—is that leaving that night became wired into me. My nervous system learned something in that moment that it has been practicing ever since. When I feel unsafe, I leave. That pattern has shaped relationships, decisions, and moments of which I am still making sense. This is what an unintegrated memory does. It doesn't just live in the past. It writes the future.

I drove home alone that night, 16 years old, trying to make sense of what had just happened. When I got home, my mom was mad at me for leaving the camp without permission. She drove me back to camp the next day and tried to force me to apologize, but I wouldn't. I didn't. My dad said he didn't remember any of it.

I spent years trying to overcome those 30 seconds. Hours of therapy. Thousands of dollars. A bachelor's degree. A master's degree. A license in clinical social work. I became a therapist, in part, as you now know, because I needed to help myself. And still, every time I thought about that night at hunting camp, I was right back there, against that trailer, my father's hands on my throat. My Dad's face was nose to nose with me as I stood watching those men do nothing.

The memory never softened. It never filed itself away. It stayed raw, present, and alive in my body, as though it had happened yesterday, no matter how many years passed or how much I understood intellectually.

Then I found EMDR.

EMDR stands for Eye Movement Desensitization and Reprocessing. My colleague Ana Gomez describes it more accurately as Eyes Moving to Digest and Recover—and that description captures it better than the clinical name ever could. When our eyes move in the specific bilateral way that EMDR uses, we sink deeper into the brain, out of the cortex, and into the parts that hold the physiological memory, what my body had been storing. That's what allowed me to finally reach the third part of my memory: my body. To move beyond just talking about it. To digest it.

For the first time, I found a way to let my body do what it had been trying to do for decades: To release the experience. To complete the cycle. To cry, to digest, to get it out—really out—and integrate the memory that my body had been holding so tightly for so long and my brain had been trying to complete.

What happened on the other side of that work was something I didn't have words for at the time.

Upon completion of that specific stress cycle, a traumatic experience, the memory didn't disappear. I didn't forget what happened. But the memory became something different; it became a story, something that had happened—not something that was still happening. I could think about that night without being transported back to it, without my body flooding, without losing days to the weight of it. The memory became neutralized, a memory in a file, in the filing cabinet of my brain, filed accurately where it was supposed to be, not floating around, easily activated.

Even as I write this, I notice the sadness. I can recognize the pain 16-year-old Stacy had to endure. But I am not sobbing. I am not wrecked for weeks. I am still not carrying this memory in my body the way I carried it for so long.

My body, my physiology, that part of my nervous system, sees it now as just something that happened to me.

That is what this chapter is about. Not forgetting. Not pretending. Not talking about it until you're exhausted. But letting your body finally do what it has always known how to do—complete the cycle, digest the experience, and file it where it belongs.

You deserve to do that with your own story and the memories that are activating you.

The Science

To understand why that healing took so long—and why it finally worked—we need to talk about how memory actually works.

Most of us think of memory as something that lives in our minds. A story we can tell. A thought we can access. A feeling we can name. And those things are part of it. But they are only two-thirds of the picture.

What EMDR training taught me—because, of course, I got training in EMDR after I experienced it as a client—in the simplest terms, was that every memory has three parts.

The first part is the thought. The narrative. The story your mind tells about what happened. This part of memory lives in the cortex—the thinking brain. It's the part most of us are most familiar with and most comfortable working with.

The second part is the feeling. The emotional experience associated with the memory. Fear. Devastation. Shame. Grief. Most of us have some access to this layer, though naming feelings precisely is harder than it sounds—it requires access to parts of the cortex that can be difficult to reach when we're activated or flooded. And we often have more than one feeling about an activating memory. That makes this second part more layered and complex.

The third part is the body experience, the physiological aspect of what occurred. And this is the part that almost nobody talks about. This is the part that most traditional talk therapy completely bypasses. And this—right here—is why so many people spend years in therapy making intellectual progress while the physiological part of the nervous system stays stuck exactly where it was.

The body experience is the physical sensation connected to the memory. For me, it was the weight of my father's hands on my neck and my shoulders. The physical pressure of that moment encoded itself in my body and stored itself there long after the event was over. That sensation had to be tied to the thoughts and the feelings—all three parts brought together—for the memory to fully integrate. Without including the body's part of the experience in my memory of it, the file stayed open.

Dr. Dan Siegel, a clinical professor of psychiatry whose work on the developing mind has shaped how we understand memory, makes an essential distinction here between two types of memory. Explicit memory is the narrative—the story you can consciously recall and tell. Implicit memory is the body memory—the sensations, reactions, and automatic responses that get encoded below the level of conscious thought, often before we even have language to describe them.

Here's what that means in practice. You can have a crystal clear, explicit memory of an event—you can tell the story fluently, calmly, in detail—and still be completely hijacked by its implicit memory the moment something triggers you. A smell. A tone of voice. A physical sensation. A situation that rhymes with the original one. The narrative is clear. But the body hasn't digested it yet.

That's why I could talk about hunting camp for years without it getting any easier. My explicit memory was perfectly intact. My implicit memory—the weight of those hands, the terror in my sister's eyes, the specific quality of that particular helplessness—was still locked in place, undigested, waiting.

When stress or trauma occurs—especially when it occurs before we have the developmental capacity to digest it, or when it's simply too overwhelming for the nervous system to digest in the moment—the memory doesn't file properly. The body experience gets locked in place. And every time something triggers that memory, the body doesn't just remember. It re-experiences.

This is also what trauma actually is—and I want to be careful here, because trauma is one of the most misunderstood words in our cultural vocabulary.

Trauma is not about the event itself. It's about the response or reaction to the event. The painful flooding that is too much for the nervous system to digest all at once.

Imagine trying to eat an entire cake in one sitting. Your body knows immediately it's too much. You can't digest it all at once. Some life experiences are like that. Something happens, and your brain and body recognize in real time that this is too big to digest all at once. So the nervous system does what it's built to do—it protects you. It stores what it can't digest. It keeps you functioning in the moment by filing the experience incompletely, with the intention of coming back to it later.

The problem is that later doesn't always come by itself.

And here's something else that matters deeply. We all have different windows of tolerance. Our nervous systems are like rubber bands—and you already know from the last chapter that some rubber bands have been stretched more than others over the course of a lifetime. A group of people could experience the exact same event, and each person's nervous system might respond completely differently. Each person's responses are valid. Trauma is not a measure of what happened. It's a measure of what the individual nervous system experienced. That's not a weakness. That's biology.

Which brings us back to the body, the physiological experience of the memory.

If memory has three parts—thought, feeling, and body experience—then healing has to address all three. Talking about what happened addresses the thought. Processing the emotions addresses the feeling. But without engaging the body, the third piece stays frozen. The file stays open. The nervous system stays on alert.

This is why I spent years in talk therapy making sense of my story intellectually while my body stayed locked against that trailer. I had the thought. I had the feeling. But nobody ever asked me about the third part. Nobody ever helped me find it, name it, or digest it.

I also want to acknowledge that the event's age matters. I was 16 in this event. My brain was not fully developed. Of course, I could access my cortex in regulated situations. One reason it can take years to fully process an event is that it may take years for our brain to be fully developed enough for processing to be possible.

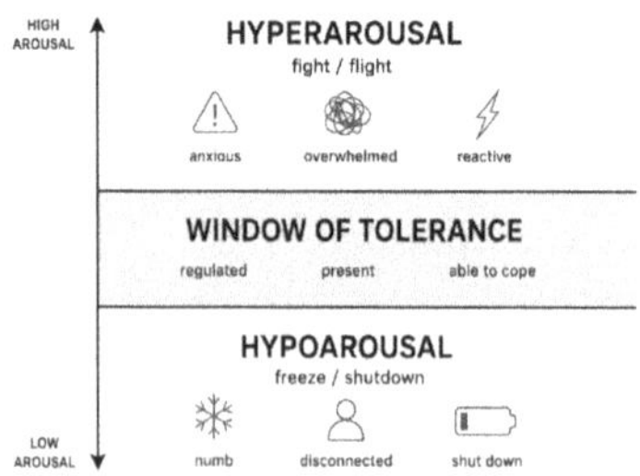

The Skill: Physiological Responses to Memory and Trauma

Before we go any further, I want you to try something small.

Take a slow breath. Let your body settle just a little.

Now bring to mind something mildly stressful—not the hardest thing you've ever been through. Something manageable. A difficult conversation. A moment of tension. An interaction that left you unsettled.

With that moment gently in mind, I want you to notice your body.

Not what you think about it. Not how you feel about it. What does your body do?

Is there tightening anywhere? Heaviness? A change in your breathing? Warmth or coolness? A sensation in your neck, your shoulders, your chest, your stomach? Something you don't quite have words for?

Just notice. That sensation—whatever it is, however subtle—is the third part of the memory. It's the piece that has been there all along, waiting to be included in the conversation.

You don't need to do anything with what you are noticing in your body right now. We're not ready for that yet—that processing comes later in this book, and we'll build toward it carefully and safely. But I want you to begin noticing that your body is always part of the story. It has been since the beginning. We're just finally going to start listening to it.

This is where real healing begins. Not in understanding what happened. In letting your body digest what it has been holding.

From My Life

Integration didn't feel the way I expected it to.

It wasn't a dramatic release or a single breakthrough moment. It was quieter than that. It felt like turning a page.

Once I was able to integrate that memory from hunting camp—once my body had finally digested what it had been holding for so long—something shifted in how I was living. I became more present. Not because the memory was gone, but because it was no longer running things from behind the curtain.

I was able to formulate appropriate boundaries with my father and my mother—not from a place of rage or reactivity, but from a place of clarity. I could focus on my own safety. I could allow myself the space to leave situations that needed to be left—consciously, as a choice, rather than as a knee-jerk reflex I didn't understand. I could listen to 16-year-old Stacy. And I could give her what she had needed all along.

That's what integration made possible—not the erasure of the past, but the ability to finally be present in my own life.

And here's what I want you to hear in that.

The work I did on that one memory didn't just resolve that one memory. It changed a lifetime of patterns that had caused me to flee every time a situation got challenging. Because that's how the nervous system works—one completed cycle creates capacity for the next. One integrated memory makes room for another. Healing isn't linear, and it isn't total. But it compounds.

You don't have to digest everything at once. You just have to start.

YOUR JOURNEY

This chapter introduced important ideas about memory, the body, and trauma. Below is a space to notice what came up for you—not to analyze or make meaning yet.

Move slowly. Pause as needed.

1. What Stood Out in This Lesson

As you learned about memory and trauma, notice what stayed with you.

This might be:

- A thought
- A question
- A feeling
- A body sensation
- Or something that's hard to put into words

You don't need to explain or connect it to anything else right now.

Reflections:

2. Memory: What Is Noticed

This chapter discussed how memory includes thoughts,

feelings, and body experiences.

As you reflect, notice anything that stood out for you about memory.

You may consider:

- Repeating thoughts you recognize
- Feelings that felt familiar
- New awareness about the body's role

Notes:

3. Body Awareness Check-In

Pause for a moment and notice your body right now.

You may notice:

- Tightness
- Heaviness
- Ease
- Warmth
- Numbness
- Or nothing at all

There is no right response.

What you notice in your body:

4. Feelings Awareness

Sometimes feelings are hard to name, especially when more than one is present.

A feelings wheel can be a useful tool to help name and identify feelings. Search "feelings wheel" to find one that is right for you.

Practice choosing a feeling and noticing your body's responses to that feeling. You can choose more than one.

Feelings you notice (or words that resonate):

5. Trauma: Personal Reflections

This chapter explored trauma as an experience of overwhelm—not an event that looks the same for everyone.

As you reflect, notice anything that came up for you about:

- Overwhelm
- Capacity
- Your window of tolerance
- Or how your nervous system has adapted

You are not required to describe details.

Reflections:

6. A Gentle Reminder

This work is about understanding—not judgment.

Write one sentence to yourself that feels supportive or grounding.

Examples:

- "My responses make sense."
- "My body adapted to protect me."
- "I can go slowly."

Your sentence:

Closing Reminder

Awareness comes before healing. Nothing needs to be changed or fixed today.

If this work feels activating, pause and return when you are ready. Your nervous system will move at the pace that is right for you.

PART TWO

Your Story

I didn't realize how far back it all went.

A NOTE BEFORE WE BEGIN

We're about to go somewhere together.

Part Two is where this work gets personal.

I have a rule that I have kept throughout my career as a therapist, trainer, and speaker. I will never ask anyone to do something I am not willing to do myself. That means every tool in this section—every list, every timeline, every question I'm going to ask you to sit with—I have done myself. In my own therapy room. With my own therapist. With my own list on my own piece of paper.

I'm not asking you to go somewhere I haven't already been.

This section is called Your Story. It's not about retelling trauma or digging for details. It's about creating a clear, organized, compassionate map of your life—so that your nervous system finally has somewhere to put what it has been holding loosely for so long.

Go slowly. Use one word if that's all you have. Stop when you need to. Come back when you're ready.

Take as much time as needed.

CHAPTER FOUR

Major Life Events

The Story

Marcus wasn't sitting in the back of the room waiting for the session to end.

He was front row, center. He had decades of experience behind him, and very few speakers had offered him something he didn't already know. But he showed up with curiosity. And that curiosity changed everything.

I have been speaking to audiences for a long time. As we discussed before, I have noticed that most people move through three stages during a training like mine.

The first stage is other-focused. They're sitting in their chair thinking about someone else—their student, their child, their spouse. The information is interesting but they think they're only learning strategies for what to do with others.

The second stage is quieter. Something shifts. They start thinking about their own childhood.

The third stage is the hardest. They start thinking about all the ways they believe they've done everything wrong. With their kids. With their partners. With themselves. This is the stage where people internalize, reflecting on their current life and how they are navigating their relationships.

The man in the front row moved through all three stages.

I was talking about stress—specifically the rubber band. I was asking people to list the events that had activated their nervous systems throughout their lives. Whatever came, in whatever order it came.

Marcus started writing.

He didn't stop.

I noticed him because of the quality of his attention—the way his pen kept moving while others around him slowed and looked up. He was somewhere else entirely. Not checked out. Checked in. Deeply, urgently, privately in.

At the end of the session, he found me.

He said, "I have sat in hundreds of breakouts where people tell me what to do. You gave me the way to do it. You told me to list the events that were activating my body. I did that, and I just kept going. I didn't realize how far back it all went."

"I didn't realize how far back it all went."

I want you to hold that sentence for a moment before we go any further. Because that man didn't discover anything I told him. He discovered something that was already there—something his nervous system had been holding, loosely and heavily, for longer than he knew. All I did was give him a structured way to look at it.

That's what this chapter is going to do for you.

The Science

There is a reason I ask people to map their lives through the lens of developmental stages rather than simply making a list and leaving it there.

You already know from Chapter 1 that the brain develops from the bottom up—brainstem first, then the midbrain, then the limbic system, then finally the cortex. Each stage of development has its own timeline. And when stress or overwhelm occurs during a particular stage, it doesn't just affect your experience of the event; it affects the part of your brain that was actively developing at that time.

That timing changes everything.

I have worked with Soldiers who enlisted at 17—before their cortex was anywhere near fully developed, before the part of the brain responsible for critical thinking, reflection, and long-term decision-making had finished developing. When those Soldiers sit down and map their timelines, something shifts. They can see it. The decision to enlist falls within the developmental window of the limbic system—the social brain, the brain most sensitive to belonging, identity, and peer influence. They weren't making a fully cortex-informed choice. They were making a limbic one. That's not a character flaw. That's neuroscience.

I have worked with teachers who, when they map their timelines, reflect on being placed in foster care at age six, right in thc middle of the midbrain stage, the window most critical for emotional development. When that teacher looks at her timeline and sees that disruption sitting in that developmental window, something clicks. The emotional regulation struggles she has carried her whole life suddenly make a different kind of sense. Her brain was interrupted during the exact season it most needed stability. That's not a personal weakness. That's timing. It carries extra weight if that teacher is a Kindergarten or 1st grade teacher and working with kids who are living life in that developmental stage. Those students are pressing on an activation button of the teacher, something below the surface, unconscious, perhaps showing the teacher what she did not receive during that developmental stage. This is a complex relational dynamic that is occurring—and without mapping out our lives, we may never have awareness about why we're being triggered.

This is why the developmental framework matters. Not to label anyone. Not to reduce a life to a chart. But because context creates awareness and awareness creates compassion. Compassion is what makes it possible to look at your own story without flinching.

Memory is not linear. And I don't want you to treat it like it is. Before we do anything with your list, I just want you to make it. Whatever comes, in whatever order it comes.

Your list will grow over time. Some stress cycles are dormant—we don't know they need completing until something activates them. Things will surface in the weeks and months after you've done deeper work. When they do, come back here. Add them. This map is a living document, not a finished one.

The Skill: Map Your Life

This exercise has two steps. Do them in order.

Step One—The List

Write about all the key events that took place in your life from in utero to your current age. Write whatever comes, in whatever order it comes. You can write a word, a phrase, or a safe label like "hard season," "medical event," or "the year everything changed." This list is yours. Nobody else will see it. There is no right way to do it, and there is no wrong thing to put on it.

Think through the full span of your life. Early childhood—what stories did your parents tell about you when you were little? Were there accidents, surgeries, or medical issues? Did your family move? Did your parents separate? What was happening before you started school?

Think about your school years—elementary, middle school, high school. Who were the teachers who shaped you, the friendships that held you, the ones that you lost?

Think about early adulthood. Relationships. Decisions. Losses. Firsts. Transitions.

Think about the big events—births, deaths, weddings, divorces. And then think about the events no one talks about at funerals or celebrates with cake but that your nervous system has never forgotten.

Write everything down. Don't edit. Don't minimize.

Pause here. Make your list before you continue.

1. Major Life Events

Begin by listing any major life events that come to mind right away.Do not worry about order yet.

You may think about:

- Births, deaths, weddings, funerals
- Moves, separations, divorces
- Accidents, surgeries, medical issues
- School experiences
- Military service, career changes
- Significant relationships
- Any other events that feel important

You are in control of how much you include.

Major events (words or short phrases only):

Welcome back.

Step Two—The Timeline

Now that your list exists, we're going to look at it through the developmental lens from Chapter One.

Take each item on your list and place it into one of the following developmental windows:

Zero to one year—brainstem development. Sensory system and survival responses.

One to six years—diencephalon development. Early emotional wiring.

Seven to 12 years—limbic system development. Social understanding, belonging, identity.

13 to 18 years—continued limbic and early cortex development. Relationships, identity, independence.

18 to 25 years—cortex development completion. Decision-making, reflection, and long-term thinking are coming fully online.

25 and beyond—the fully developed brain, navigating the accumulated experiences of everything that came before.

Approximations are fine. Just notice where things land. Notice which developmental windows feel full. Notice which ones feel empty.

We're not interpreting yet. We're gathering.

We'll add one more layer to this map in Chapter 7. For now, just let the list be what it is.

2. Timeline: Placing Events by Developmental Stage

Now, gently place the events you listed into the age ranges below. You may repeat events if needed, or leave sections blank.

In utero–nine months

One–six years

Seven–12 years

12–18 years

18–25 years

25–present

From My Life

Context matters.

My father's violence toward me when I was 16 at hunting camp, and my realization about alcoholism at 18 at college were both experiences that happened when my full thinking brain was not developed. I got married when I was 21, also without a fully developed brain. This gave me additional context when my marriage ended.

As I became a mother, I held the understanding of my children's developmental stages. My divorce gave my children their own ACE score. And the context for them also matters. They experienced divorce at ages 8 and 9, during a critical period for emotional development. This context gave me a way forward in supporting them and understanding the impact that significant event had on their development.

Once we map our own lives, we can begin to show compassion as we reflect on the lives of our loved ones: our children, spouses, siblings, and parents. Context matters when it comes to development and the experiences that happened during our development.

Your Journey

Your list exists now. Your timeline is taking shape.

This chapter is about creating a clear, organized map of your life—not reliving events or digging for details.

You are not required to describe experiences in depth.

Move slowly. Pause as needed.

3. Noticing

As you placed events into the timeline, notice if anything stood out.

This might be:

- Surprise
- Curiosity
- Emotion
- Neutral awareness
- Or nothing at all

There is no right response.
What You noticed:

4. Body Check-In

Before moving on, pause for a moment and notice your body.

You may notice:

- Calm
- Tension
- Heaviness
- Ease
- Fatigue
- Or nothing noticeable

What you notice in your body right now:

Closing Reminder

This list is a map—not a demand.

You do not need to process or change anything yet. If this feels activating, pause and return when you are ready.

You are moving at the right pace for your nervous system.

You made your list. That took courage.

CHAPTER FIVE

What the Main Events Overshadowed

The Story From My Life

For years, when I thought about hunting camp, I recalled only onc thing: My father's hands on my throat. That was the headline. That was what my nervous system led with every single time, without fail—the 30-second moment that overshadowed everything else so completely that everything else simply didn't exist yet, couldn't exist yet. My nervous system didn't have room for anything else.

A shift happened, but it took time. Significant time. And it happened in layers, not all at once.

Once the headline was integrated and had somewhere to live, the next thing to surface was my mother. She had driven me back to camp the next day and tried to force me to apologize. I remembered that factually for years as part of the story I could tell. But my feelings about what my mother asked of me were different. Feeling this meant sitting with the question I hadn't yet been able to ask: why wasn't my mother protecting me?

That question, when it finally arrived, carried its own weight and caused its own activation and gave it its own place on the list.

As I've worked through this, I've come to understand that my mother was protecting herself. A person does not access the logical parts of the brain when experiencing abuse, thus, it seems like there is no logic available to explain these behaviors. My mother and I have had many repairing conversations over the years. We have healed, together, the trauma we both experienced that day. But that healing couldn't begin until I could first feel her betrayal. And I couldn't feel her betrayal until the headline had been integrated.

My sister surfaced next. Not the image of her face at camp, which I had always carried. But now I had the capacity for a fuller understanding of what her experience had been. She is also a therapist now, which tells you something about the paths that certain childhoods create. What I came to understand, over time, was that her relationship with our father had always been different from mine. She was more partner than daughter—a terrible position for a child to be placed in, and one she navigated with a kind of survival intelligence that I couldn't see clearly while I was still managing my own headline.

She stayed at camp that night because she knew the fallout of leaving would be worse for her. That was not a weakness. That was her nervous system making the most accurate calculation it could in that moment. Two sisters. Same parents. Same event. Same night. Completely different experiences—and completely different wounds that needed completely different healing.

The last thing to surface took the longest.

The men.

I was a grown woman—married, with children of my own—sitting around a campfire with my husband and a group of our friends, men and women, when it landed. One of the men in our group had too much to drink. My nervous system was activated, alert, ready to protect. And then, the other men intervened. They stepped in. They saw something happening and did something about it, helping get that man to bed, away from the bigger group of people. And in that moment of safety, surrounded by men who showed up, my nervous system reached backward across decades and quietly added something to the list.

The men at hunting camp didn't intervene.

Not just in that moment. Not in any moment. For years.

That detail—the silence of those men—had been there all along, filed somewhere behind the headline, waiting until I had enough safety and enough capacity to feel it. It arrived not as a crisis but as a clarity. A piece of the picture that had always been true, finally visible.

That's how closing these stress cycles works. These could be trauma events or events where your body is activated. Secondary stress cycles (or traumatic events) don't disappear while the headline is loud. They wait. And when the headline finally has somewhere to live, they begin, quietly and on their own timeline, to surface.

This chapter is here for when they do.

The Science

Your nervous system is extraordinarily intelligent.

When something overwhelming happens—something that activates the brainstem, that floods the body with stress hormones, that demands every available resource just to get through the moment—your nervous system makes a decision. Not consciously. Not deliberately. But with the precision of a system that has one primary job: to keep you alive and functioning.

When you later recall that overwhelming incident, your focus will be on the most activating thing. In my example, the most activating part of the memory was my dad's hands.

Everything else gets overshadowed. The other parts of your memory aren't deleted or lost. They're just set aside, waiting for a season when there is enough capacity, enough safety, enough settled ground, for you to notice them and examine them more closely. The secondary part of my memory was my mom and sister. I couldn't notice those pieces until my dad's hands on my throat, the most activating part of the memory, had been dealt with.

This is why two people can be at the same event and have completely different experiences. You already know from Chapter 3 that we each have a different window of tolerance—a different rubber band, stretched differently by different histories, with different amounts of capacity available in any given moment. What one nervous system can digest in real time, another has to file for later.

My sister and I were at the same camp on the same night. We both carry that night. But we carry different parts of it, weighted differently, shaped by nervous systems wired differently by our different positions within the same family. Neither of our experiences is more valid than the other. Neither of our healing journeys looked the same.

This plays out in therapy rooms every day.

I have worked with many clients navigating religious trauma—and I want to name that clearly, because it is not named enough. Religious trauma is real. It causes specific kinds of suffering, and it deserves to be called what it is.

Dr. Dan Siegel offers a phrase I return to often: name it to tame it. When we give something a name—when we move it from a vague, shapeless weight into a word we can say out loud—we engage the cortex in a way that helps regulate the nervous system. Naming is not just semantic. It's physiological.

So, religious trauma.

For many clients I have worked with, their headline, the part of their religious experience that most deeply traumatized them, was purity culture—the specific, pervasive messaging that their bodies were dangerous, that their sexuality was shameful, that their worth was tied to their physical purity in ways that no young person should ever have to carry. That headline was loud. It shaped how they understood themselves, their bodies, their relationships, and their faith.

And once we began to address that deep trauma—once that headline had somewhere to live—everything it had overshadowed began to surface.

Self-esteem that had been quietly eroded. Relationship roles shaped by theology rather than genuine choice. Communication patterns built around silence and compliance. A complicated, grief-filled relationship with faith itself.

Purity culture is one face of religious trauma. It shows up in many forms—shame around doubt, spiritual abuse, the performance of belief rather than the experience of it. Whatever form it took in your life, if it shaped your nervous system, it belongs on your list.

There are many clients I've worked with in therapy who had experiences like mine. An event occurred (war trauma, sexual abuse, bullying) and once that event had been digested, once all three parts of the memory (feelings, thoughts, and body sensations) had been filed, then they had the capacity to deal with the other parts connected to that event. I often tell my clients clearing the headlines is like pulling out the really big weeds that we know are there. Once the giant weeds are pulled out, there is space to see what else is happening: Are there smaller weeds to pull? Is there more capacity to see what else is in the soil?

The point is this. Whatever your headline has been, whatever your nervous system has been leading with—there are surely other things behind it. This chapter exists to hold those things. And it will hold them for as long as you need—whether that's now, or months from now, or after the deeper work in

Part Four has given the headline somewhere to finally live.

The Skill: The Quieter Stressors

This exercise works the same way as Chapter 4, with one important difference.

We are not looking for the main events here. We are looking for everything they overshadowed.

Think about what was happening around the main events on your list. Recall the people who didn't show up or showed up in the wrong way. Remember the silence that followed something loud or the apology you were asked to make, even though you didn't owe one. Reflect on what happened the day after, or in the quiet months that followed a crisis.

Think about the accumulation—the everyday experiences that didn't make headlines but that your nervous system registered nonetheless. Maybe you lived with chronic low-grade stress in a home that never felt quite safe. Maybe you experienced crushing loneliness that doesn't have a single point of origin. Perhaps you endured the slow erosion of something—confidence, trust, a sense of belonging—that happened so gradually you didn't notice until it was gone.

Think about the messages you received—about your body, your worth, your gender, your role, your faith, your identity.

Write what you can see right now. And then—leave space.

This list is a living document. It has no deadline. It will grow on its own timeline, in its own seasons, as your nervous system develops the capacity to surface what has been filed behind the headlines. You may add nothing to it today and find three things waiting for you six months from now, after you have done the work in Part Four and the headline has somewhere to live.

Come back here then. Add the new discoveries you've unearthed. This page will be waiting.

1. Everyday Stressors and Triggers

Begin by listing everyday experiences that create irritation, tension, or activation for you.

These might include:

- Household tasks or clutter
- Traffic or driving
- Crowded or noisy environments
- Work interruptions or demands
- Technology issues
- Feeling rushed or behind
- Interactions that drain your energy

There is no such thing as a stressor that is "too small" to list.

Everyday stressors (words or short phrases):

2. Patterns You Notice

As you look at your list, notice if anything stands out.

You might notice:

- Repetition
- Similar themes

- Situations that activate you quickly
- Stressors you tend to minimize

You do not need to make meaning of this yet.
Notes:

As you build your list, place each item into the same developmental timeline from Chapter 4. Hold what you find with curiosity.

Don't ask yourself, "What is wrong with me that I didn't see this before?"

Ask, "From what was my nervous system keeping me safe until now? What was I being protected from?"

3. Timeline: Chunking Everyday Stressors

Now gently place these stressors into the developmental timelines below. This is not about when the stressor first occurred—it's about when your nervous system may have learned how to respond.

Leave sections blank if nothing comes to mind.

In utero–nine months

One–six years

Seven–12 years

12–18 years

18–25 years

25–Present

Your Journey

This chapter focuses on everyday stressors and quieter life events. These experiences may feel small or "just part of life," but they can still activate your nervous system.

You are not required to explain, analyze, or fix anything. Use short words or phrases only.

Move slowly. Pause as needed.

4. Body Check-In

Pause for a moment and notice your body.
You may notice:

- Tightness
- Restlessness
- Fatigue
- Calm
- Neutral awareness

There is no correct response.
What you notice in your body right now:

Closing Reminder

Everyday stress still counts.

You are not being asked to change anything yet. This journaling practice is about noticing patterns—not fixing them.

If this feels activating, pause and return when you are ready. You are moving at the pace that is right for your nervous system.

CHAPTER SIX

PEOPLE, PLACES, AND SPACES

THE STORY

It was March 2025, and I was in Erbil, Iraq.

I was there visiting Soldiers from my unit—two of them had been stationed there long enough to know the environment well. They suggested we go into downtown Erbil for dinner, away from base, out on the economy, the way you do when a place has become familiar enough that you feel safe in it.

During my daily call with my husband, I mentioned the plan.

My husband's reaction was immediate and strong. He was adamant. "Stacy, I am not supportive of you going. This isn't safe. Do not go. Something could happen. This is not a risk I am comfortable with. Not a good plan." I must not go. I should not leave the base. Danger was out there, he was certain of it. The position in which he held his body and the tone of his voice conveyed the urgency he felt; his feelings came through the phone from thousands of miles away.

I knew exactly what was happening.

My husband had done years of significant therapeutic work regarding his time in Iraq, careful, intentional work that had addressed the main events. That work was real, and it had mattered. He had been seeing a therapist who did Brainspotting, a more client-centered approach with similarities to EMDR.

But nobody could have predicted that his wife—me—would be in the location where he had experienced so much trauma. A new layer, uncharted, arrived without warning, 19 years after his original experience. His nervous system didn't file it under "my wife is having dinner downtown." It filed my dinner plans in the same folder that held everything else that location had ever meant to him. The folder labeled threat-danger.

That's not a failure of his healing. That's the nervous system doing exactly what nervous systems do—protecting the people we love using the only maps they have.

I respected his wishes. Calming his stress response mattered more to me than dinner somewhere that felt threatening to him, so we stayed on base. I did not go and I am okay with that. Some may read this as a controlling partner, but I knew that was not at all what this was. This was an activated nervous system of someone concerned about his wife. I want to make this distinction because these dynamics occur thousands of times a day in relationships and are often misunderstood.

But before we ended the call, I said something to him that I want to say to you now.

"Because of your sacrifices and your trauma, this town is safe enough to eat in, for now."

I meant it as a gift—a reframe, an acknowledgment, a way of holding his pain and his healing in the same sentence. What he had lived through had contributed, in some small way, to a world where his wife could walk those streets safely. His wound had a legacy beyond the wound itself.

Still, the echoes of our trauma remain for many years with those who love us.

Places hold things. Not in the walls or the streets or the geography itself—but in the nervous system of every person who has moved through them carrying something significant. A location becomes a file. And sometimes that file gets activated not because you yourself have returned to the site of the activating event, but because someone you love is there.

This chapter is about mapping those files. The places your body remembers. And the people—the ones whose names, faces, roles, or absences have left a mark on your nervous system that is still, in some way, shaping how you move through the world.

The Science

My son once said to me—with the particular honesty that teenagers reserve for the people with whom they feel safest, "Mom, why would I want a relationship with you? You are the most complicated relationship in my life."

I chuckled.

And then I said, "My dear son, moms are the most complicated people in everyone's life. It's literally why I have a job."

He was right, of course. And so was I.

The people who reliably activate our nervous systems are almost never strangers. They are the people we are closest to—the ones whose approval we needed earliest, whose presence shaped the most critical windows of our development, whose words landed in us before we had any defenses against them.

I want to pause on something about children and the word no. We don't want children who simply comply. Compliance without internal assent is what we produce when we prioritize obedience over relationship. And a child who learns to comply—to override their own internal signal in order to keep the peace—is a child who may not be able to access that signal when they need it most. When a stranger asks them to do something that feels wrong, when a partner crosses a line, or when their own body is telling them something, they may feel unable to act in their own best interests.. We don't want children who automatically comply. We want children who are safe enough to disagree—and who practice that disagreement first with the people who love them.

The list of people who activate our nervous systems doesn't stop with parents. It extends outward in ways that can surprise us and may include a teacher who humiliated you in fourth grade, a coach who made you feel simultaneously essential and invisible, a friend you outgrew, a boss whose approval you chased for years without understanding why, an ex-partner, or a person from your past who died before your relationship could be repaired.

And sometimes our nervous systems are activated by losses that don't have official names.

A few years ago, a boy I had dated as a freshman in high school—someone I had loved in the uncomplicated way you love when you are a teenager—died by suicide. He was a junior when we dated. By the time he died, more than 20 years had passed. He had built a full life and been married for decades with several kids and grandchildren. I had spoken to him exactly twice in all those years between high school and his death.

And yet, when I heard the news, my body reacted with a deep feeling of weight in my chest, a numbness that washed through me, a heavy feeling for which I didn't have a category.

What I lost wasn't a current relationship. What I lost was the keeper of a memory—the only other person who had been present for a specific chapter of my life, someone who held his side of a story that now existed only on my side. He existed in a part of my brain development very particular to social relationships, feelings of love and acceptance, and the individuation that teenagers go through. My grief over his death was palpable, but the world offered no container for it. No casserole. No bereavement leave. No socially sanctioned space to grieve over someone I hadn't spoken to in decades.

My nervous system didn't care about the current relationship status. It cared about what he had meant to me. And the stress cycle that opened when he died needed to be completed—whether the world recognized my grief or not.

This is why the people section of your map needs to be as wide as your actual experiences—not as wide as what the world considers a legitimate loss.

Dr. Dan Siegel's work reminds us that our nervous systems are shaped in relationship. We are wired for connection from the very first moments of life—the brainstem developing in utero, already attuned to the heartbeat of the person carrying us, already learning what safety and threat feel like from the inside of another human being's body. The people who were present during our critical developmental windows didn't just influence our memories. They helped build the architecture of our nervous systems.

And places—as my husband's Iraq story shows—can hold that same neurological weight. A location becomes associated with a nervous system state. The body recognizes it. And sometimes the recognition happens so deep, so early, or so completely that the place itself becomes a trigger long after the original experience has passed.

My hometown did that to me for years. I left at 18 and never returned to live there. But when I came back to visit, my body had its own opinion about the trip. I spent my visits sneezing, aching, and having a runny nose. Eventually, I was evaluated at the Emergency Room for pleurisy—an inflammation around the lungs brought on by what the doctors ultimately identified as a stress response. My body was trying, in the most physical terms available to it, to keep me from returning to a place where I'd endured so much harm..

Once I understood what my body was reacting to—once I could name what that place held for my nervous system—my response began to shift. That's what naming does. That's what mapping does. That's what this chapter is for.

The Skill: People, Places, and Spaces

This exercise has two parts. Do them in order, and do them the same way you've done every exercise in Part Two: Make a written list with no judgments and no editing, just writing whatever comes up for you in whatever order it comes.

Part One—The People.

Think across your entire lifespan. Zero to now.

Who has activated your nervous system—for better or for worse? Who stretches your rubber band? Who, when you think of them, produces a response somewhere in your body before your mind has even finished forming the thought?

Start with the obvious ones. Parents. Caregivers. Siblings. Then widen. Teachers. Coaches. Friends. Former partners. Bosses. Colleagues. People you loved and lost. People you lost before you could love them the way you wanted to. People whose absence shaped you as much as their presence did.

Include losses without official names. The person who died before you could repair what was broken between you. The person with whom you were in a relationship that ended without resolution. The person for whom you felt grief, even if the world didn't recognize your right to grieve. If your nervous system felt activated by someone, something, or somewhere, it belongs on your list.

1. People or Roles

Begin by listing people or roles that have activated your nervous system at any point in your life.

These may include:

- Family members
- Romantic partners

- Friends or peers
- Authority figures (teachers, coaches, supervisors)
- Medical providers
- Strangers or brief interactions that left a mark

You are in control of what you include.

People / roles (words or short phrases only):

2. How Old Were You? (Age or Age Range)

For each person or role you listed, write down how old you were—or the age range you were in—when you were in relationship with them.

Exact ages are not required. Approximations are enough.

Person / Role—Age or Age Range:

3. Timeline: Ordering by Developmental Stage

Now, gently place these people or roles into the developmental timelines below.

This is about noticing when your nervous system learned certain relational responses—not about assigning blame or meaning.

Leave sections blank if nothing comes to mind.

In utero–9 months

One–six years

Seven–12 years

12–18 years

18–25 years

25–Present

Part Two—The Places and Spaces.

Now think about locations. Towns. Schools. Workplaces. Medical buildings. A specific room. A car. A natural environment. Anywhere that triggers a response in your body before your mind catches up.

Think about the places you avoid without fully understanding why. Think also about the places that feel like relief. Safety has a geography, too.

List the places. Note your approximate age when you were there.

Once both lists exist, place each person and each place into the developmental timeline from Chapter 4. Just notice where things land.

We're not interpreting yet. We're still gathering.

4. Places and Spaces

Begin by listing places or spaces that create—or have created—activation for you.

These might include:

- A town, neighborhood, or hometown
- A school, workplace, or medical building
- A specific room or house
- A car or type of vehicle
- A coffee shop, store, or public space
- A natural environment

Include only what feels accessible today.

Places / spaces (words or short phrases only):

5. How Old Were You? (Age or Age Range)

Next to each place or space you listed, write how old you were—or the age range you were in—when you spent time there.

Exact ages are not required. Approximations are enough.

Place / Space—Age or Age Range:

6. Timeline: Ordering by Developmental Stage

Now, gently place these places and spaces into the developmental timelines below.

This is about noticing when your nervous system learned certain responses—not about assigning meaning or blame.

Leave sections blank if nothing comes to mind.

In utero–nine months

One–six years

Seven–12 years

12–18 years

18–25 years

25–present

From My Life

I want to tell you what I noticed in the weeks after finally understanding what my hometown held for my nervous system.

Something had shifted. Not in the circumstances—the history was still there, unchanged. But in me. The file had been named. And named things can be worked with in ways that unnamed things cannot.

Your nervous system has stored all of the things that happened to you, whether anyone else was watching or not.

Now we're just writing it down.

YOUR JOURNEY

Your people list and your places list exist now. You've done the mapping. Now let's notice what you found.

This chapter focuses on people, relationships, places, and spaces that have activated your nervous system.

You do **not** need to use real names. You may identify people by role only (for example: parent, teacher, partner, supervisor, stranger).

You are not required to describe interactions or relive experiences. You are not required to explain why a place or space feels activating or describe what happened there. Short words or phrases are enough.

Move slowly. Pause as needed.

7. Noticing

As you organized this information, notice if anything stood out.

You might notice:

- Repetition, certain ages or stages repeating
- Clusters around certain ages
- Familiar roles
- Strong body responses to specific environments
- Or nothing at all

There is no right response.

Write what you noticed:

8. Body Check-In

Before moving on, pause for a moment and notice your body.

You may notice:

- Tension
- Heaviness
- Calm
- Fatigue
- Neutral awareness

All responses are valid.

Write what you notice in your body right now:

Closing Reminder

This list is a map—not a judgment.

You are not being asked to confront anyone, make any decisions, nor change anything yet. This journaling practice is about awareness and organization.

If this feels activating, pause and return when you are

ready. You are moving at the pace that is right for your nervous system.

CHAPTER SEVEN

YOUR ACTIVATION SCALE

THE STORY

I had been gone for six months. This was my first deployment. It was my husband's first time being left behind—though not his first deployment. He had deployed three times before I did, which meant he knew something about me that I didn't yet know. He had watched, from the leaving side, what extended time away does to the person who stays. And now, with the roles reversed, he understood what was coming home inside me better than I did.

We had carefully planned my return home. We'd had lots of conversations and had done lots of planning. We'd agreed he would take the first week off when I returned. We had talked through those details, discussed them, and agreed on them. What we had not discussed was the second week I was home. In my mind—in the mind of a woman whose nervous system had been running on a six-month stretch with none of her normal anchors—the second week was obvious. Of course, he would stay home again. Of course!

When he mentioned going back to work that second week, my activation went from zero to ten in approximately fifteen seconds.

My face went hot. My breathing changed. My whole body

started shaking. Tears came before I had any words for what was happening. And in those fifteen seconds, somewhere between the activation and the words, I had already imagined divorcing him. I had separated our houses, divided our finances, figured my way out. I was leaving—putting into play my good ol' patterns of running away coming back to save me. The planning was that fast and that complete—because that's what an activation of ten does when it arrives in a nervous system that has been stretched for six months with no dogs, no bed, no Colorado sunshine, no good water, no kids, no husband, and no anchors. I'd had nothing I normally used to release my rubber band, and it showed in my immediate reaction to my husband.

My regulation tools before deployment were simple and specific. My dogs. My own bed. The Colorado weather and sunshine. Good water—I know how that sounds, but my body knows the difference. Being home. My kids. My husband. Those were my anchors. All of them, together, kept the rubber band at a manageable stretch and release.

For six months, I'd had none of them. And my nervous system had been compensating—holding it together, doing the job, functioning—the way nervous systems do when they have to. Competently. Quietly. At significant cost.

And then came the planning of returning home. And one small miscommunication about one week of leave detonated everything that had been held together for six months.

My husband heard the activation in my voice and left work. He told me, "I am leaving work because this phone call needs to happen at home. I will call you as soon as I get home."

That act alone—him getting in the car—began to release the stretch, to regulate me. Not because the problem was solved, but because someone I trusted was taking my reaction seriously. He was coming toward me instead of moving further away. In the eight minutes it took him to drive from his office to our home, I finished divorcing him in my head and started to feel the first edges of something that wasn't quite panic anymore.

He called from home. And he said—calmly, clearly, without meeting my 10 with his own—"Babe, if you had told me you wanted me to take the second week off, I would have. We never even discussed this. You never gave me a chance to fix it."

My activation dropped nearly immediately.

I was still stretched. Six months of accumulated stress didn't disappear in a phone call. But my husband's words did something specific and precise to my nervous system. His words were true, and they were fair. He delivered them without anger, without retaliation, without escalation. He didn't meet my 10 with his own. He drove home. He stayed regulated. And his regulation co-regulated me.

I felt safe, seen, and grateful—deeply, specifically grateful—that he didn't give me what I gave him.

I also recognized, in the aftermath of that activation, something important. I had leaned into old patterns. The impulse to leave—to create the exit before the conflict had even been addressed—that was familiar. That was my nervous system reaching for the tool it had learned decades ago in a hunting camp parking lot. The tool that had kept me safe once was in the filing cabinet, ready to be accessed as needed.

Deployment had stretched my rubber band so far that my window of tolerance had narrowed. And in that narrowed window, old patterns had been reactivated. Not because I needed to work through the initial event again. Because I was in a new situation, with minimal regulation tools, I reached for a known skill that worked to get me through the stress that was taking over me.

That's what an activation level at 10 does. And that's exactly why understanding your activation scale—really understanding it, personally and precisely—matters more than almost anything else in this work.

The Science

Understanding activation is an important part of understanding your brain, your stress cycle, your stress reactions, and your healing. This part is hard work. I know that. Take your time. We are using our cortex to organize your healing and get you ready for completing stress cycles.

Learning about the activation scale, which is what we're talking about in this chapter, created growth for me in really big ways because it gave me a common language for what was happening in my body.

Activation is what happens when our nervous system starts to feel the stress—the stretch of that rubber band. Activation doesn't mean something is wrong; it simply means that your nervous system is alert, responding. So the activation scale runs from zero to 10. Zero means no activation. Ten is fully activated. The scale is very personal.

For me, a one looks like my foot tapping. A 10ten looks like I am leaving a situation in a dysregulated, unpredictable, emotional state. I'm not behaving in a healthy way, just falling back on my old modus operandi. I was at a 10 when I was divorcing my husband in my mind as he drove home to call me.

Everything between zero and 10 gives you information.

Your goal is awareness, specifically awareness early enough to make a choice.

When I noticed my activation in that phone call, I was already at a 10. The choice had already been made by my nervous system before my cortex had a chance to weigh in. That's what 10s do—they bypass the thinking brain and act from the survival brain. By the time you're at a 10, you're not choosing your response. Your nervous system is choosing it for you, based on the best available information it has, which is usually decades old.

The intervention—the place where awareness actually changes outcomes—happens at the lower numbers. At a three. At a four. Before the survival brain takes the wheel.

This is why I use numbers instead of feeling words when I talk about activation. Feeling words require access to the cortex—they require you to identify, label, and articulate an emotional state. When you're activated, that access is compromised. But numbers are simpler. Numbers live lower in the brain. Most people can tell you they're at a six even when they can't say exactly what they are feeling or why.

Dr. Bruce Perry's work on the Neurosequential Model reminds us that we cannot access the higher functions of the brain—empathy, reflection, problem-solving, nuanced communication—when our lower brain is running on high activation. We have to regulate first. Then we can relate. Then we can reason. In that order. Always in that order.

This is why the scale matters. Not as a measurement of how bad things are. As a tool for knowing when to regulate before you respond.

Progress in healing is not measured by whether you still reach a 10. Most people who do this work still reach their 10 sometimes. What changes is three things—and when all three shift, you are making real progress.

Frequency. How often does the ten arrive?

Duration. When the 10 arrives, how long does it last?

Severity. When the 10 arrives, is it still as consuming as it once was?

When frequency, severity, and duration are all impacted—even slightly—healing is happening. That's the measure. Not perfection. Not the absence of activation. The gradual shift in those three dimensions over time.

My 10 still looks like it always has. The difference is that it arrives less often, recovers faster, and doesn't always reach the same ceiling it once did. That's not a cure. That's progress. And progress, in this work, is everything.

The Skill: The Activation Scale

Understanding your personal activation scale is one of the most practical things you will do in this entire book.

It starts with anchoring the ends.

What does zero look like for you? Not a fantasy of perfect peace—your actual baseline. The version of you that is settled, resourced, and present. Where are you? What's around you? What does your body feel like? For me, zero looks like being home. My dogs nearby. Good water. Colorado light coming through the window.

What does 10 look like for you? Not the worst moment of your life—just full activation. Your nervous system completely online. What happens in your body? Where do you feel it?

Once you have the ends, build the middle.

What does a one feel like? A two? These are the early warning signs—the foot tapping, the slight tension in the shoulders, the small irritability that arrives before you've consciously registered that something is wrong. These are the numbers that matter most, because these are where intervention is still possible.

Work your way up slowly. Write it down. Make it specific. Make it yours.

Now, reflect on your lists from the previous chapters. Give each of your events, each of your stressors - events, people, places, and spaces - a number. How activated are you when you think about these stressors? There is no right or wrong answer. And the activation may change from day to day. Just start noticing. Pause. We are creating awareness. Going through this intentional inventory makes a huge difference in your own healing.

This may take a few days. Or you may chunk this into more

manageable sections. Don't push yourself beyond what you are ready for. Listen to your nervous system and take your time.

As you complete this exercise, imagine that each of your activation numbers is a brick. The events that carry a 10 are 10 bricks. The events that carry a two are two bricks. Over a lifetime, you can see that all of those events with each of those activation scales are a whole lot of bricks. That's why your capacity, your window of tolerance, is limited. That's why things feel heavy. Perhaps you are numb. Perhaps you are reacting more strongly than the situation warrants.

In the therapy room, this begins to show clients why life feels harder than it did before. Over and over, stress cycles open, bricks weighing things down.

If you feel comfortable, you can share this information with your loved ones. "When I am activated at a one, I start tapping my foot. You may notice me tapping before I do. Please help me with my awareness."

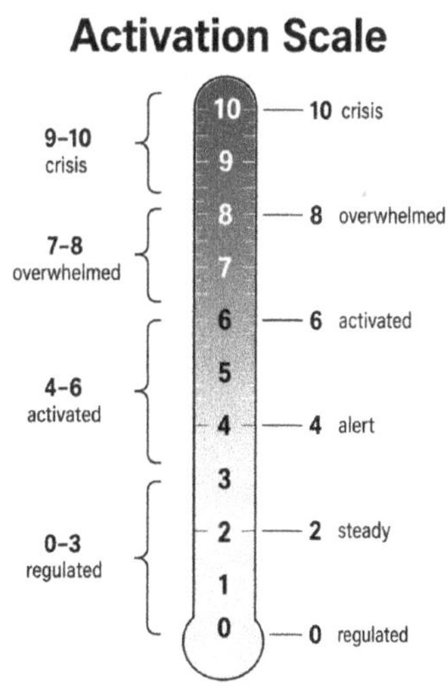

From My Life

I want to repeat what my regulation tools actually look like. Not the clinical version—the real one.

My dogs. My own bed. The specific quality of light in Colorado—the way the sun comes through at altitude, different from anywhere else I've lived. Good water. Being home. My kids. My husband.

That's it. That's the list. No five-step morning routine. No elaborate protocol. Just the specific, ordinary, irreplaceable things that my nervous system has learned to associate with safety over the course of a life.

When all of those things are available to me, my activation is low. When they are removed—as they were for six months of deployment—the baseline shifts. The rubber band starts the day already stretched. And the window of tolerance narrows until even a small miscommunication can become a detonation.

What I want you to hear in that story is not that I failed. I didn't fail. My nervous system did exactly what it was built to do—it reached for the most reliable protection available, the one it had been practicing for decades, and it did it fast.

What I want you to hear is that awareness came. Maybe not in the fifteen seconds before the activation. But in the aftermath, when my husband's words landed, and the scale came back down, I could see it clearly. I could name what had happened. I could recognize the old pattern running. And I could say—out loud, to him—you're right. I never gave you a chance to fix it.

That moment of awareness is what the scale makes possible. Not prevention—not always. But awareness. And awareness, in this work, is where everything starts.

He knew what to do with my activation because he had

been watching it, carefully and lovingly, for years. He had deployed three times and had stood on the leaving side long enough to understand what the returning side felt like. When the roles reversed, he used that knowledge to take care of me.

That's a support system. Not someone who prevents your 10. Someone who knows what your 10 looks like—and drives home anyway.

Your Journey

This chapter introduces the Activation Scale, a simple way to notice how intensely your nervous system responds to stress.

Using a scale—rather than feelings language—often makes stressors more tangible, easier to manage, and easier to work with. You do not need to find the "right" emotional words. Numbers are enough.

Move slowly. Pause as needed.

1. Understanding Your Activation Scale

The activation scale runs from 0 to 10.

- 0 = no activation at all

- 10 = fully activated

This scale is personal. Your numbers may look different from anyone else's.

Take a moment to define a few anchor points for yourself.

A low level of activation (1–2) looks like:

A mid-level activation (4–6) looks like:

A high level of activation (8–10) looks like:

2. Adding Activation Numbers to Your Lists

Now, return to the lists you created in the previous lessons:

- Major life events
- Everyday stressors
- People
- Places and spaces

Next to each item, add an activation number from 0–10.

You may notice:

- Some items feel mildly activating
- Some feel very activating

- Some surprise you

There is no right or wrong number.

Notes / Examples (optional):

3. Patterns You Notice

As you add activation numbers, notice if anything stands out.

You might notice:

- Certain categories have higher numbers
- Activation clusters around specific ages
- Some "small" stressors carry high activation
- Or nothing at all

All responses are valid.

What you notice:

4. Body Check-In

Pause for a moment and notice your body right now.
You may notice:

- Tension
- Ease
- Fatigue
- Curiosity
- Neutral awareness

There is no correct response.
What you notice in your body right now:

Closing Reminder
Activation is information, not a problem.

You are not being asked to reduce, fix, or change anything yet. This journaling exercise is about creating clarity so future work can be done safely.

If this feels activating, pause and return when you are ready. You are moving at the pace that is right for your nervous system.

PART THREE

Resourcing and Building Safety

Support is the lifeline to healing.

CHAPTER EIGHT

SUPPORT PEOPLE AND SAFE SPACES

THE STORY

I was in my National Guard office one day when a senior enlisted Soldier knocked on my door.

He had a junior enlisted Soldier with him. I will call him Jake. The junior Soldier looked defeated, his shoulders slumped, avoiding eye contact, clearly stressed out. The senior Soldier was angry—face red, voice tense.

He said, "I need you to talk to this guy. He really screwed up, and we need to determine whether we should kick him out or keep him."

I agreed to talk with him. I asked the senior Soldier to leave my office, but he refused. He said he was afraid the Jake would get violent with me.

I want you to sit with that for a moment—not because the senior Soldier was wrong to be concerned—he wasn't, not entirely. But because this was a display of the most common human response to behavior that has gone sideways: Fear meeting fear, authority meeting dysregulation with more threat. Jake had already been brought to the edge and was now standing in front of two people—one angry, one waiting to evaluate whether he was worth keeping.

This is what happens in schools. In homes. In workplaces. When someone's behavior becomes too big for the container they're in, the people around them respond with tightened control, ultimatums, and decisions made about a person who isn't yet in the room.

After much insistence, the senior Soldier left. And it was just the two of us.

We sat there in silence for a bit. I shared a little about myself and my background. Then I asked him how old he was.

He was nineteen. Just a kid.

Jake made some poor choices during Annual Training. He'd had a fight with another Soldier and wrecked a military vehicle. He was in serious trouble. But I knew, from everything my clinical training had taught me, that a person does not just wake up and have behavior problems.

As my friend and colleague Bryan Post says: All behaviors arise from a state of stress. Somewhere between stress and behavior is either love or fear.

This young man was in a state of fear. So I did what I do when people are scared. I started to talk about the brain. ACEs (childhood traumas). His nervous system. Stress cycles. I educated him on things he had never heard about before he walked through my door.

We were together for about two hours. Much longer than he ever expected.

At the end of those two hours, we found out that Jake had an ACE score of 10. He had zero support outside of the military. And he loved the military with everything he had.

Jake was a traditional National Guard Soldier. His service commitment was one weekend a month and two weeks of Annual Training a year. He told me about a cycle he had noticed—that he could keep it together while he was at home, in between drills, but during drill and Annual Training, he would come completely unglued. He would drink and get violent. He would express his big anger and take it out on everyone around him. He didn't understand why he was acting out this way. He felt shame. His behavior was costing him the one thing in his life that mattered.

I understood it immediately.

I tell parents all the time that kids have the biggest feelings with the people with whom they feel safest. This young man was safe when he was at drill and Annual Training. He finally had people around him who could hold space for what he was carrying. And his nervous system, which had been white-knuckling it alone for nineteen years, finally felt safe enough to let out all those big feelings.

He didn't have a behavior problem. He had a nervous system that had never had a container large enough to hold him. And the military—imperfect, institutional, sometimes clumsy in its response—had accidentally become the first safe place he had ever known.

He needed the military. Not just for the structure or the paycheck. For the belonging. For the first experience of his life of people showing up consistently, of a community that didn't leave.

At the end of that first session, we agreed on a safety plan. We agreed on regular counseling. As he began to understand what an ACE score of 10 actually meant—what it explained about his history, his patterns, his nervous system—he started to understand why he acted the way he did. And he started to understand that he needed more support than he had ever allowed himself to ask for.

I agreed to answer every call. No matter what time. No matter what day.

We began to build his support system together—mostly military people, the community that had already become his anchor—and slowly, carefully, he began to heal.

Fast forward two years.

He was healthy and stable enough to deploy. He knew that deployment would offer something he had never reliably had before—a regular paycheck, access to a gym, three meals a day prepared by someone else. The basic scaffolding of a regulated life, finally available to him. He was excited.

Fast forward three months after he landed in the Middle East.

He had no idea I was joining that deployment.

When I got to the base, I found that young man and hugged him like he was my own son.

One hug. Two people, a world away from home. That one act represented so much love and support through a tumultuous time in a young man's life.

Support is the lifeline to healing.

The Science

According to Google, co-regulation is the process by which one person's calm, regulated nervous system helps another person feel safe and emotionally balanced. Co-regulation is necessary for the human experience. We were created to live in tribes, where co-regulation is naturally present and where we had people around us to provide empathy, attunement, and presence. Throughout evolution, our "tribes" have become much smaller, and we live in much smaller support systems with families of three to six, often without extensions of aunties, uncles, and grandparents.

This chapter is about understanding, recognizing, and building the support system we should have naturally, but often do not.

One person cannot meet all of our relational needs. So, we must look at who is in our corner. Who can we count on? Who can we trust? Who is showing up for us in a non-judgmental manner? Who is safe? For some of us, we may have several people. For others, we may need to intentionally build this. We need a mutual exchange of emotional support to survive this world.

That's science. That's biology. Before we can have self-regulation, we must have co-regulation.

We also heal in relationships. Intentionally evaluating our relationships is important for the work that you are doing.

Safety is important to this process. It's a part of the science. Felt safety is that deep, internal feeling of knowing that you are safe, all of you. For some people, this felt safety is created in the relationships with their biological families. For some of us, that felt safety did not exist within our families of origin. As we take inventory of our relationships, safety must be part of the discussion.

I also want to address professional support; there is an implication that professional relationships are somehow less real, less valuable, or less intimate than personal ones. I don't believe that. Some of the most regulated, most genuinely non-judgmental, most carefully attuned relationships in a person's life are professional ones. You can find genuine support with a therapist, a spiritual director, a mentor, or a sponsor. These relationships are built specifically to hold what personal relationships sometimes cannot—and there is no shame in leaning on them heavily, especially in seasons when your personal relationships are stretched or insufficient.

Professional support and personal support are not competing categories. They are complementary ones. A healthy support system often includes both. This matters for how you build your support system. The people in it—professional and personal alike—need to be people whose presence actually regulates you—not people who should be able to regulate you, and not people who have the right credentials or the longest history with you. You need people whose presence actually produces regulation in your body. That's the test.

So, when you think about support people, consider safety and co-regulation.

Let's discuss safe spaces.

Our sensory system develops early in life. Our first encounter with the sensory-system experience is in utero, in the womb of our biological mothers. Before we were born, we were encased in amniotic fluid, listening to the heart rate of our mother, hearing her voice, the vibration of her internal systems. If our mother is safe and regulated, our sensory system becomes safe and regulated. If our mother is living in that stretched-out state of dysregulation, our sensory system feels that, too. Throughout our development, we have various sensory-system experiences that either support our nervous system or dysregulate our nervous system. Some of us are more sensory sensitive. Some of us have stronger filters and can tolerate overwhelm. This impacts us long-term.

As we navigate this chapter, I encourage you to get curious about your own sensory system and what is supportive of our emotional and relational regulation.

The Skill: Support People and Safe Spaces

Take an honest inventory.

Not an aspirational one—not the support system you think you should have—but the one you actually have right now.

Think about the people in your life with whom you can be completely safe and honest, where the full, unedited truth of your experience would be received without judgment, without redirection, without the relationship becoming smaller or more fragile as a result.

If your primary person became unavailable tomorrow, who

else is in your system? Where are the gaps? You don't need to fill them immediately—but see them clearly. And think about professional support. Is there someone in your life—a therapist, a spiritual director, a mentor—who is specifically equipped to hold what your personal relationships cannot? If not, is that a gap to which you should be attending?

Think about your physical and sensory-support system. The places, sounds, textures, and environments that actually settle your nervous system. Running water. A specific kind of light. A physical practice. A song or sound. Don't underestimate these; they are not luxuries or indulgences. They are legitimate, evidence-based components of a functioning regulation system.

Use the journaling practices in this chapter to create a safe space, real or imagined. This will anchor your nervous system, your sensory system, as we navigate the stressors that we have identified.

A support system doesn't have to be large to be sufficient. Quality matters more than quantity. Two or three relationships of genuine depth, a few sources of physical regulation, a safe space, and access to professional support when needed is enough. That is, in fact, what many of the most regulated people I know are working with.

From My Life

When my first marriage ended, I quickly discovered who my people were.

This discovery wasn't dramatic the way a crisis sometimes reveals character with grand gestures or middle-of-the-night calls, with seeing which friends show up with food and stay for hours. The discovery was quieter than that, more specific. What I discovered was not who loved me. I already knew that. What I discovered was who could hold space for me.

There is a difference.

Kaydi answered every call. Every single one. She didn't always have answers. We didn't always have deep, meaningful conversations. What she had was presence—the irreplaceable presence of someone who could sit with me in the middle of the hardest season of my life without needing it to be over, without needing me to be better, without needing my discomfort to resolve itself into something more manageable.

"I'm here, and I'll listen. You're going to get through this."

That's what she said. She didn't say, "I know exactly what you're going through." Or, "Here's what you should do." Or, "I'm sure it will all work out." She just gifted me with her presence, was a witness, and provided the radical and underrated act of staying on the phone with me.

She changed what that season felt like. Not what it was—the divorce was still the divorce, the losses were still the losses, the nights were still the nights. But the experience of moving through it was different because someone was genuinely there.

I want to tell you something else about that season, because I think it matters for this chapter.

I moved into a mountain home with a creek. On purpose.

Not just because it was beautiful—though it was. But because my nervous system needed what running water provides. Water that moves, moves energy. I had known that clinically for years, and now I put it into practice for myself. I would sit by that creek and just let the sound do what sound does—regulate, settle, remind the nervous system that the world is larger than the immediate crisis. Running water provides bilateral auditory stimulation. Proximity to natural environments consistently reduces cortisol. My body knew this before my mind did.

A couple of years later, I also got a water rower for the same reason. The rhythm, the movement, and the bilateral quality of the pull helped me intentionally build a regulation system into my physical environment.

This chapter is about building a full ecosystem of support--not just the people, though the people matter enormously. A healing nervous system requires a supportive environment along with supportive people.

Build your system around good people who can show up for you, and show up for the people you love in that same way.

Your Journey

This chapter focuses on identifying people and spaces that can support you during your healing journey. You are not being asked to change anything today—only to notice what support already exists and where there may be space to build more.

Move slowly. Pause as needed.

1. Personal Support People

Begin by listing people in your personal life who feel supportive, safe, or nonjudgmental.

These might include:

- Family members
- Friends
- Members of a faith or community group
- Acquaintances you feel comfortable around
- People you'd like to deepen your connection with over time

Use names or roles—whatever feels safest.

Personal support people:

2. Professional Support People

Next, think about professional support in your life.

This might include:

- A therapist or counselor
- A pastor or spiritual leader
- A mentor or coach
- A medical provider
- Another professional whose role is to support you

If you don't currently have professional support, that's okay. You are making these lists simply to build your awareness.

Professional support people:

3. Your Safe Space

Answer any of the prompts below that feel supportive. You do not need to answer them all.

Your safe space may be:

- A real place you've been before
- An imagined place
- A combination of both

If a safe space doesn't come to mind right away, that's okay. Sometimes safety is something we build gently over time.

Pause as needed.

Where do you feel safe?

Is this space real, imagined, or something you're creating?

Is it indoors or outdoors?

What is the environment like? (weather, light, sounds, movement)

What do you need around you to feel safe here?

4. Anchoring This Space

If it feels helpful, consider one small detail that helps you remember this space.

This might be:

- A word
- An image
- A color
- A sensation

A detail that anchors my safe space:

5. Noticing Gaps (Without Judgment)

This chapter also focuses on noticing gaps in safety—areas where support, stability, or ease may feel limited.

Gaps in safety are common, especially among people who have lived through hard or unsafe experiences. They are not a failure. They are information.

You are not being asked to fix anything today.

Move slowly. Pause as needed.

As you reflect on your support people, safe spaces, and resources, notice if any gaps come to mind.

A gap might feel like:

- Limited or absent support in one or more categories
- Feeling unsure to whom you can reach out
- Not having a place that feels fully safe
- Wanting more support but not knowing where to start

You do not need to label this as “good” or “bad.”

Gaps you notice (words or short phrases only):

6. Protection, Not Failure

Take a moment to remember: your nervous system learned to protect you.

Some gaps exist because narrowing your world once helped you stay safe.

How protection may have shown up for me:

7. Curiosity Instead of Urgency

Instead of asking what's missing, gently ask what might help—when and if you're ready.

You may reflect on any of the questions below. You do not need to answer all of them.

- What would help me feel a little safer?
- Would this support be personal or professional?
- Would it be a person, a place, or a practice?
- What would make expanding safety feel more manageable?

Gentle reflections:

8. Capacity Check

It's possible to want more support and not yet have the capacity for it.

That's okay.

Right now, my capacity feels like:

9. Body Check-In

Pause for a moment and notice your body.

You may notice:

- Calm
- Tension
- Relief
- Fatigue
- Neutral awareness

All responses are valid.

What you notice in your body right now:

Closing Reminder

Support is something we build over time.

It's okay if your list feels short.

It's okay if it looks different from what you expected.

Gaps in safety do not mean you are behind.

They mean your nervous system learned how to protect you.

Nothing needs to change today. Awareness is enough.

We will continue building safety slowly and intentionally throughout this module.

CHAPTER NINE

GROUNDING AND THE BODY

THE STORY

I was fifteen years old, standing on a ridgeline in Hell's Canyon.

We had ridden four-wheelers out to the edge—my family, my dad sober that day, the kind of day that complicated everything because it reminded you of who he could be when he wasn't who he usually was. As we stood there looking out over miles of canyon that seemed to go on forever, something happened in me that I didn't have words for at the time.

My body went both completely calm and completely anticipatory at once. Calm because the scale of it—the sheer scale of standing on the edge of something that vast—made the noise inside me quiet. Small problems couldn't find purchase in a view like that. The nervous system, confronted with something that enormous and that still, simply let some things go. Anticipatory because I felt, in my body, that something was possible. Not a specific something. Just—I had a sense of vast possibility and felt the particular quality of aliveness that comes from being somewhere beautiful with no ceiling and no walls.

I didn't know then that I was grounding. I didn't have that word. I just knew that I needed to find ways back to that feeling. That it was something I would spend my life returning to.

That ridgeline has been with me ever since.

Grounding is the skill that makes all the other skills possible. It is the foundation beneath everything in Part Four of this book. And it looks different for every nervous system, which is part of why this chapter asks you to do some discovery, rather than handing you a single technique and telling you it will work.

The Science

There is a grove of aspen trees on the land where I live now.

I didn't know, when I chose this property, that those aspens would become one of the most important metaphors in my entire career. I just knew that when I looked at them, something settled in me that doesn't always settle.

Here is what I know about aspen trees now that I didn't know then. The trees you see above ground are not individual organisms. They share a single root system—a rhizome that runs beneath the surface of the soil, connecting every trunk to every other trunk in the grove. What looks like a forest of separate trees is a single living entity, continuously sending up new growth as older trunks age and decline.

The Pando clone in Utah is one of the most famous examples—a single aspen organism estimated to weigh 13 million pounds, covering more than 100 acres, possibly thousands of years old. Individual trees come and go. The root system persists.

I think about that when I think about generational trauma. The roots run beneath the surface, beneath what we can see. Individual trunks grow from those roots, shaped by what the roots carry. And when one trunk finally grows in a new direction—when one person in a family system does the healing work and breaks the pattern—the roots are still there. The new growth is still connected to everything that came before.

What looks like separateness is connection. What appears

individual is shared. Breaking a generational cycle doesn't sever the roots. The same root system now accommodates something growing differently.

We'll come back to that in the conclusion of this book. For now, I want to stay with the grove.

Grounding, in the clinical sense, means giving your nervous system something real and present to anchor to when activation is pulling you toward the past or the future. Grounding is a bottom-up regulation strategy—meaning it starts with the body, with sensation, with the brainstem and the sensory system, rather than with the thinking mind.

When your nervous system is activated, your cortex is largely offline. You cannot think your way back to baseline—not reliably, not quickly, not when the activation is significant. But you can feel your way back. You can give the sensory system something to orient to in the present moment—a texture, a temperature, a sound, a physical sensation—and the nervous system will use that anchor to begin returning to baseline.

This is why grounding techniques work. Not because they are tricks or distractions. But because they speak directly to the part of the nervous system that is running during activation—the brainstem, the sensory system—in a language that part of you can understand.

Grounding looks different for every nervous system. The key is to find what actually works for you, not what should work, not what works for the person next to you in yoga class. What actually produces settling in your specific body?

Some people ground through sight, through envisioning a specific view, or a color, or a natural environment that the nervous system associates with safety.

Some ground through sound, through imagining running water, or listening to a specific kind of music, or through letting silence descend, or by hearing the sound of their own name said by a person they trust.

Some ground through touch, through rubbing a specific texture between their fingers, through setting the temperature just where they need it to be, through the weight of a blanket, or by feeling their hand on a solid surface.

Some ground through movement, through the bilateral rhythm of walking, or the feel of their body caught up in dance, or the specific quality of a physical practice that the nervous system has learned to associate with regulation.

I want to say something specifically about the voice of a guide in body-based practices. Your nervous system has to trust the voice before it can relax into it. If a guided practice puts your body on higher alert rather than lower—if the voice creates tension rather than releases it—that is not a failure of the practice. That is your nervous system giving you accurate information about what it needs. Trust that. Keep looking until you find a voice that your body will fccl comfortable following.

The Skill: Grounding

This skill has two parts—one for when you are regulated and one for when you are not.

When you are regulated—when you are at a two or a three on your activation scale, not in the middle of a crisis—I want you to go looking for your grove. Your ridgeline. The specific sensory experiences that produce genuine settling in your body.

Where does your nervous system go to settle? What does it look like? Sound like? Feel like?

Start collecting these grounding details, not as a list of what should settle you, but as a gathering of what actually does. Your body already knows. You're just beginning to listen to it on purpose.

When you are not regulated—when the scale is climbing,

and you need an anchor —I want you to use what you've collected.

One technique I return to often is what I call the five-four-three-two-one grounding practice. Name five things you can see, four things you can touch, three things you can hear, two things you can smell, and one thing you can taste. This is a sensory inventory—it gives the brainstem something concrete in the present moment to which it can orient itself, which helps interrupt the nervous system's pull toward the past or the future.

But this sensory inventory is just one option. Your version might sound like running water, or feel like the weight of a specific blanket, or a short walk with attention on the alternation of your feet, or music playing bilaterally (more on that in Chapter 15), or aa texture you hold in your hand, or a view you can always recall.

Build your grounding toolkit from the actual materials your nervous system responds to. And practice it when you're regulated—not just in the moments of crisis. The nervous system learns through repetition in all states. Practicing when you're calm builds the muscle. Practicing when you're activated allows you to use it. You need both.

From My Life

I drove to the courthouse on a day that mattered.

I was going through my divorce. There were hearings. There were moments that required me to be present and regulated in rooms where being present and regulated was almost impossible—rooms where the stakes were high and my activation was predictable, and I needed something that would carry me through the door without having me fall apart on the other side of it.

I put on Eminem.

Not because Eminem is the most soothing option available. But because the driving, relentless bilateral rhythm of his music—the way it moves between left and right, the sheer insistent forward momentum of it—did something specific to my nervous system. It organized me. It gave my activation a container. It said to my brainstem, in the only language my brainstem could hear in that moment: here is rhythm, here is pattern, here is something to follow.

I got out of the car regulated. Or regulated enough. That's all I needed.

Grounding doesn't have to be serene. It doesn't have to look like meditation, nature walks, or gentle breathing. Sometimes it looks like Eminem in a courthouse parking lot.

Find what works for your nervous system. Use it without apology.

And know that the ridgeline will be there when you need it. Whatever your version of it is.

Your Journey

Grounding and visualization are skills that help your nervous system return to the present moment.

These practices are not about forcing calm or relaxation. They are about offering your body moments of safety and support.

You are always in control. Pause or stop at any time.

1. Grounding: Coming Back to the Present

Grounding uses your senses and your body to help you orient to the present moment.

Take a moment and gently notice:

What you can feel supporting your body right now (chair, floor, bed, ground):

Something you can see in the room:

Something you can hear:

Any physical sensation you notice (warmth, tension, ease, neutral):

2. Visualization: Imagining Safety

Visualization invites your brain to imagine a place, experience, or sensation that feels steady or safe.

You do not need to see images clearly. Some people sense, feel, or simply know.

Answer any prompts below that feel supportive.

Your safe or steady place is:

What feels safe or comforting about this place:

Details you notice:

- Light/weather/temperature:
- Sounds or quiet:
- Objects, nature, or surroundings:

3. Body Awareness

As you ground or visualize, pause and notice your body.
You might notice:

- Slowing
- Relaxation
- Tension
- Neutral awareness
- Or nothing at all

All responses are valid.
What you notice in your body right now:

4. When This Might Be Helpful

Grounding and visualization can be used at many points throughout the day.

You might try these practices:

- At the start of your day
- Before or after a stressful interaction
- When your activation begins to rise

- As part of a nighttime routine

Times when grounding or visualization might help:

5. Tools To Explore:

Some people find guided supports helpful when practicing grounding or visualization.

You may explore:

- Calm App
- Insight Timer
- Headspace
- Short grounding videos or audio

These are supports—not requirements.

Notes or tools you might try:

Closing Reminder

Grounding and visualization are practices you can return

to again and again.

You don't need to do them perfectly. You don't need to do them for long.

Even small moments of safety matter.

Use what works. Leave the rest.

PART FOUR

The Release

You have done something significant. You mapped your story.

A NOTE BEFORE WE BEGIN

You have done something significant.

You mapped your story. You looked at the major events, the things the headlines overshadowed, the people and places that shaped your nervous system, the activation that has been running in the background of your life. You gave all of it a number. You built a picture of what your nervous system has been holding—and you did it without being asked to relive anything, without being pushed past what felt safe, without anyone else in the room telling you what your experience meant.

That took courage. And that map matters.

Part Four is where we learn what to do with "it." "It" refers to feelings, thoughts, sensations, and the abstract ways that your nervous system (your brain and body) will show up in these exercises. Everyone's "it" is different. Some people will have visuals. Some people will have sensations. Some people will have feelings or thoughts. There is no wrong answer. The answers are as individual as the people who are reading this book.

The skills in this section—just notice, sit with it, acknowledge and notice and release, make it tangible, decide what to do with it, give your nervous system a rhythm to hold—are not abstract exercises to be practiced in a vacuum. They are tools built specifically to help you work through what you mapped. Your list from Part Two is the material. These skills are how you begin, gently and at your own pace, to complete the cycles that have been waiting.

I want to be clear about something before we begin. You do not have to start with the hardest thing on your list. You do not have to work through everything. You do not have to finish. There is no timeline here, no grade, no finish line you need to cross by a certain date.

What I am asking you to do is start. Choose one thing from your list—something for which you feel ready, something that carries a real charge but not an overwhelming one—and bring it into the practices ahead. Let the skills do what they were built to do. Trust the process more than you trust your fear of it.

I have sat across from thousands of people who were exactly where you are right now. People who had done the mapping and were standing at the edge of the actual work, wondering if they could do it. Wondering if it was safe. Wondering if anything would actually change.

Every single one of them was more capable than they knew.

So are you.

When you're ready—and only when you're ready—turn the page.

CHAPTER TEN

JUST NOTICE

THE STORY

Stella was 14 years old and had a wide range of emotions that day.

This was not unusual. Stella has always had a wide range of emotions—she came into the world fully formed in that regard, with big feelings that arrived fully and immediately, without apology. This is one of the things I love most about her. It is also one of the things that requires the most of me as her mother.

But on this particular day, I was tired. Stretched. Running on less capacity than I wanted to bring to mothering. And the particular quality of her emotions that afternoon was loud enough to reach the places in me that I work hard to keep from being reached.

I felt the pull. Not to yell—I've done enough of my own work that yelling is rarely where I land anymore. But to leave. To remove myself from the room, to put some distance between her activation and mine, to find some space where the noise couldn't follow me.

I went upstairs.

I sat in my rocking glider.

I drank a glass of cold water.

And I waited.

Not because I had given up on the conversation. But because I had enough awareness in that moment to know that nothing useful would happen between us while I was at an eight. I needed to come down first. My brainstem needed something to hold before my cortex could come back online. The rocking. The cold water. The rhythm. Bottom-up regulation was chosen consciously because I knew what would happen if I skipped it.

Somewhere in those minutes of rocking and hydrating and breathing, something came back online. I was able to remember a clinical truth I know in my bones but sometimes need my regulated nervous system to access: children only share big feelings with the people with whom they feel safe. Stella's emotions were allowed to be as big as she needed them to be because I was a safe person for her. Her activation was not a threat. It was evidence of trust.

She was bringing hcr hardest feelings to the person she believed could hold them.

That reframe changed everything. I didn't go back in with a solution or a speech. I just went back. Present. Settled enough to be present. We gave each other space. We connected again over dinner. Both of us were more regulated by then, and our repair was quiet, ordinary, and real.

That's it. That's the whole story. Not dramatic. Not triumphant. Just—a woman sitting in a rocking chair long enough for her brainstem to settle, so that she could go back and be the mother her daughter needed.

Just taking a moment to notice when you're activated can make all the difference. Just notice.

The Science

Viktor Frankl—psychiatrist, Holocaust survivor, author of *Man's Search for Meaning*—wrote something that has stayed with me since the first time I encountered it:

Between stimulus and response, there is a space. In that space is our power to choose our response. In our response lies our growth and our freedom.

That space. The gap between what happens and what we do about it.

"Just notice" is how we find that space.

Here's what neuroscience tells us about what happens in activation. When your amygdala—the alarm system of your brain—detects threat, it initiates a response in approximately twelve milliseconds. One one-thousandth of a second, faster than a blink of an eye. Before you have consciously registered what is happening, your brainstem is already reacting. Your heart rate is changing. Your stress hormones are releasing. Your body is reacting, protecting.

By the time you are consciously aware that you are activated, the response is already underway. This is why we react before we think—not because we are impulsive, immature, or lacking willpower. But because our alarm system is twelve milliseconds fast, and the thinking brain is significantly slower.

The goal of Just Notice is not to prevent the alarm from going off. It is to develop the awareness to recognize, as early as possible, that the alarm is sounding. And that recognition—even a few seconds earlier than usual—changes what is available to you.

"Just notice" is the beginning of that practice for you too. Not suppression. Not compliance with yourself. Honest, curious awareness of what is actually happening in your nervous system, early enough to make a choice about what comes next.

The Skill: Just Notice

Just notice is exactly what it says.

Not judge. Not fix. Not immediately respond. Just observe—with curiosity and without urgency—what is happening in your body when activation begins to build.

Take one item from one of your key events from above. Something that is activating. Something that is also manageable. Read that item. Think of that experience. Then, Just Notice.

What do you notice first? Where in your body does activation arrive first? For some people, they feel it in the chest—a tightening, a heaviness, a change in breathing. For others, it's the jaw, the neck, or the stomach. For others still, it's a sensation they don't have words for yet—a kind of fullness or heat or the particular quality of a held breath.

Start there. Just notice that.

Then notice the number. Where are you on your scale? Not to judge the number—just to know it. One to ten. Approximate. Right now.

Then notice the thought that arrives with the activation. Not to analyze it or dispute it—just to see it. Let yourself observe what is interesting, that this is where your nervous system goes. Imagine your thoughts floating through your mind like water flows down a river. Just notice the thought. Just notice the feeling.

None of this has to happen out loud. None of it has to be shared. It is an internal practice of awareness—building the muscle of noticing so that, over time, you can access that space between stimulus and response just a little more reliably.

From My Life

The phrase that catches me most often—the one that tells me I'm in a Trainwreck of the Unconscious™ moment—is something like: my mom or dad just came out of my mouth. I've coined (and trademarked) this phrase because it resonates so much with what I see happening in the therapy room.

The Trainwreck of the Unconscious™ is the moment you become aware that you've been living out the exact patterns from your own childhood—the things that frustrated you most about your parents, the behaviors you swore you'd never repeat—running in your own life right now, without your awareness. The collision between who you intended to be and what you've been unconsciously doing has arrived.

I swore I would never say certain things. I knew, clinically, why those things were harmful. I had spent years helping other people identify and interrupt those patterns.

And then one day, in the middle of a conflict with my daughter Stella, I heard one of those things come out of my mouth.

Not loud. Not dramatic. Just—there. In my voice. With my face. Wearing my words.

I stopped.

I felt the shame land—quick and specific and familiar. Not because I am a terrible mother. But because the Trainwreck of the Unconscious™ doesn't care about your clinical training. It runs below the level of awareness, shaped by ten thousand interactions from childhood, moving faster than your best intentions can follow.

I went back to Stella. I said—I just heard something come out of my mouth that I have no business saying to you. That was not okay. I'm sorry.

I didn't make a long speech nor provide an explanation of my childhood that made it her job to understand me. I acknowledged my mistake and offered a a repair.

She looked at me and said, "It's okay, mom."

And I said, "It's not okay. But thank you for forgiving me. And I'm working on it."

That is what "just notice" makes possible. Not perfection. Not the permanent elimination of old patterns. The awareness, early enough to stop, to see what happened, and to go back.

Your Journey

This journaling exercise supports the skill of "just noticing."

You are not being asked to change, fix, analyze, or understand anything. You are simply observing what is already there.

If at any point this feels overwhelming, pause. You can return to grounding or resourcing at any time.

1. Settling Into the Practice

Before writing, take a moment to settle your body.

You may choose to:

- Sit comfortably

- Feel your feet on the floor

- Notice the surface supporting you

When you're ready, begin.

2. Just Notice – Right Now

Without judgment or evaluation, notice what is present in this moment.

You do not need complete sentences. Words or short phrases are enough.

What thoughts do you notice right now?

What sensations do you notice in your body?

What do you notice in your environment (room, light, sounds, objects)?

3. Just Notice – In Daily Life

Over the next 24–48 hours, practice noticing in everyday moments.

You may jot things down as they arise or return later to reflect.

Something you noticed when you woke up:

Something you noticed during the day (work, home, errands, traffic):

Something you noticed when you felt tired, hungry, or overstimulated:

4. Examples of Noticing:
If helpful, noticing might sound like:

- "I notice my shoulders feel tight."
- "I notice my stomach clenches here."
- "I notice my body softens around this person."
- "I notice my breath changes."

There is no need to go further than this.

5. Body Check-In
Pause for a moment and notice your body now.
You may notice:

- Ease
- Tension

- Neutral awareness
- Fatigue
- Or nothing at all

All responses are valid.
What you notice in your body right now:

Closing Reminder
Noticing is information.

You are not required to act on what you notice. You are not required to understand it.

When we notice the thing, the thing simply is.

Take as much time as you need with this practice before moving on.

CHAPTER ELEVEN

Sit With It

The Story

It was a Tuesday morning, and I was on a yoga mat.

I was in the middle of my divorce, and the process was harder than I ever could have imagined. My friend Meg had convinced me to try hot yoga—not my usual style, not what I would have chosen for myself in that season, but she was persistent in the way that good friends are when they know you need something you haven't figured out yet.

The room was hot. Deliberately, aggressively hot. The instructor started the yoga session by saying, "Today we are going to do some trauma-informed yoga poses. These poses allow your body to release what it has been carrying." I took a deep breath and noticed the irony of being in that class. I knew all about trauma-informed yoga. I am a trauma-informed speaker, trainer, and clinician. I buckled up emotionally for what was about to happen.

On the second pose, I started crying, the soft, gentle cry that begins the release. On the third pose, I started ugly crying. The full, unglamorous kind of crying that happens when something that has been held very tightly finally finds a way out. I sat on my mat, no longer trying to participate in the poses. And, right there, right then, I made a decision. I would sit on this mat for the next 90 minutes, because, of course, it was an extended class, and I would let my body release. In a room full of strangers, I ugly cried as I sat crisscross applesauce. And I added bilateral tapping to that ugly crying and just sat with it.

Meg was there. She didn't try to stop it. She didn't look alarmed or embarrassed. She stayed on her mat, and she stayed present, and she let it happen. She offered a look of reassurance and then continued with her yoga practice.

After the class ended, the instructor came over. She checked in with me to see if I was okay. She was also curious about the tapping. I took the time to give her some trauma-informed clinical education. I said, gently: "When you offer these trauma-informed poses, you need to be prepared for people to break wide open in this room. The bilateral tapping allows the person to fully digest the experience and lets the brain complete some of the stress cycle that has been opened." She was appreciative for the information.

That particular room—the heat, the movement, the bilateral quality of the practice, the physical demand that took my cortex fully offline and let my body do what my body had been trying to do for months—gave me something that all the conversations and all the processing and all the sitting in a therapist's office had not given me. The hot yoga class was an environment where something that had been held could finally be released.

I was grieving five things simultaneously that morning, and I knew it even then. The eighteen-year marriage itself. The ACE score I was adding to my children's lives by divorcing, over which I was feeling the particular guilt of a therapist who knows what that number means. The loss of my best friend, who had been my husband, before he became someone I was leaving. The future I had imagined and would not have. The dreams that had to be revised.

Five griefs. One yoga mat. One friend who stayed.

Emotions are like ocean waves. Sometimes they tickle your toes. Sometimes they knock you completely off your feet. But they always recede. That morning, several waves knocked me over. And every single one receded. By the time I walked out of that room, I was not fixed. I was not done grieving. But something had shifted. And something that has moved is different from something that hasn't.

That's "sit with it." You don't solve it. You don't eliminate it. You let it move through.

The Science

Dr. Pat Ogden's work on somatic experiencing gives us an essential clinical framework for what I'm about to describe.

The body stores our experiences. We established that in Chapter 3. When an experience is too overwhelming to digest in real time, the nervous system files it incompletely—in sensation, in the body, in the implicit memory that has no narrative but has plenty of physical reality. That storage is not a failure. It is the nervous system doing its job, protecting you from more than you can take at a time.

But stored material doesn't stay inert forever. It exerts pressure. It looks for completion. It shows up as activation that seems disproportionate to the current moment, as physical symptoms that baffle doctors, as emotional responses that arrive faster and stronger than the situation seems to warrant.

"Sit with it" is the practice of staying with that pressure long enough for it to move.

You don't need to sit with it long enough to resolve it entirely—that's not what one sitting accomplishes. Nor do you need to sit long enough to analyze it or understand it fully—that's the cortex's job, and the cortex needs to wait its turn. You just need to sit long enough for the wave to crest and begin to recede. Just long enough for your nervous system to learn—through direct, body-level experience—that the hard feeling will not kill you. That it has a beginning, a middle, and an end. That it is survivable.

This is harder than it sounds, because most of us have spent years—sometimes decades—getting very good at *not* sitting with it. Our off-ramps are efficient. Our avoidance strategies are practiced. The moment something uncomfortable begins to build, the reflex to reach for an off-ramp is fast, automatic, and feels completely reasonable.

"Sit with it" asks you to interrupt that reflex. Not permanently—not to abandon your off-ramps entirely, which would be overwhelming and counterproductive. But temporarily. Just long enough to let the wave do what waves do.

Dr. Ogden's work reminds us that the body's completion process has its own timing and its own intelligence. We do not direct it. We do not control what surfaces or when. We create the conditions—safety, permission, a regulated enough container—and then we get out of the way and let the body do what it knows how to do.

The conditions matter. A hot yoga room worked for me because the heat and physical demand of extended poses took my cortex offline, giving my body permission to lead. Bilateral tapping on the mat helped my nervous system stay with what was moving rather than shutting it down. The presence of a trusted person there and not trying to fix anything provided the co-regulation that made it safe enough to let the wave come.

Your conditions will look different from mine. The temperature, the movement, the level of privacy, the kind of support present—all of that should be tailored to what your nervous system needs. The practice is the same: stay long enough for the wave to move.

The Skill: Sit With It

Choose something from your list of events. You can either choose a key event or something that was overshadowed. You don't need to choose the hardest thing, but pick something with a real charge—enough that you can feel it when you bring it to mind, but not so much that it floods or overwhelms you.

Bring this experience gently into your awareness. Let yourself feel the edges of it—not the full weight, just the edges. A small amount of contact.

And then—stay.

Just notice what the body does with that contact. Ask your body what it needs. Where does the sensation arrive? What does your body want to do? Does your body want to tighten and protect? Does something want to release?

If something internally wants to release—let it. Cry if crying comes. Shake if shaking comes. Breathe more deeply if breathing comes. These are not signs that something has gone wrong. These are the stress cycle completing, the wave moving through.

If nothing comes—that's also okay. The body completes on its own timeline. Some sessions of "sit with it" produce movement, and some produce stillness. Both are valid. The practice is the same: create the conditions and stay.

I also want to say something important about bilateral support during this practice. Alternating taps—left hand, right hand, left knee, right knee—can help the nervous system stay with the experience rather than flooding or shutting down. The bilateral rhythm gives the nervous system something to hold while the material moves. We'll explore this more fully in Chapter 15, but if you have a bilateral music playlist available, this is a good practice to do while letting bilateral music play quietly in the background.

And practice sitting with a traumatizing memory when you are regulated, too—not just in the hard moments. Building the capacity to stay requires repetition in all states. The more familiar your nervous system is with the experience of sitting with something hard and surviving it, the more accessible that capacity becomes when activation is high.

From My Life

I want to tell you what I learned on that yoga mat that no training had taught me.

Grief does not care about your timeline.

I knew that clinically. I had sat across from hundreds of people in the midst of losses of all kinds and offered them the clinical truth that grief has no schedule, no prescribed stages, no appropriate duration. I believed it. I taught it.

And then I was the one on the mat, and what I understood intellectually became something I knew in my body. Five griefs at once. All of them real. None of them patient. None of them was interested in whether this was a convenient time or a controlled environment.

The room did what it did. The wave came. I stayed. I intentionally chose to stay. I knew the value of "sit with it."

And the staying—the simple, unglamorous act of staying on the mat and letting the wave move through—was the most useful thing I did for my own healing in that entire season. Not the conversations. Not the analysis. Not the clinical understanding of exactly what I was experiencing and why. The staying.

Meg was there. And the instructor laid a hand on my back. And I didn't have to be okay for either of them.

That's the support system doing exactly what it's supposed to do.

Your Journey

This journaling exercise supports the practice of sitting with something you have already noticed.

You are not required to stay with anything that feels overwhelming. *You are always allowed to stop.*

This practice works best in short windows (1–3 minutes).

1. Choosing What to Sit With

Choose one small, manageable thing you have already noticed.

This might be:

- A mild physical sensation (tight shoulders, headache, shallow breath)
- A low-level emotion
- A subtle stress response

This is not the time for your hardest experiences.

What you chose to sit with (words or short phrases only):

2. Sitting With It (1–3 Minutes)

As you sit with this experience:

- Breathe slowly
- Do not analyze

- Do not judge
- Do not try to change it

Simply allow it to be present.
You may stop at any time.
3. Just Noticing While You Sit
If helpful, gently notice:
What do you notice in your body?

Did anything shift, soften, or change—even slightly?

You do not need to notice a change for this practice to be effective.

4. Returning to Safety

When you're ready, bring your attention back to the present.

You may:

- Feel your feet on the floor

- Look around the room
- Take a slow breath
- Return to a safe space

How you helped your body settle afterward:

5. Body Check-In
Pause and notice your body now.
You may notice:

- Neutral awareness
- Relief
- Fatigue
- Calm
- Or nothing at all

All responses are valid.
What you notice in your body right now:

Closing Reminder

Sitting with something is not endurance.

Short moments count. Stopping counts. Returning to safety counts.

You are learning to stay—without forcing.

That is enough.

CHAPTER TWELVE

Acknowledge, Notice, Release

The Story

Sidney sat across from me in my counseling office and told me she was afraid her son was going to kill her.

He was nine years old.

She was not an unreasonable woman. She was not fragile, dramatic, or prone to catastrophizing. She was a mother who had opened her home and her heart to a child with a significant trauma history—a child who had been internationally adopted, who had experienced things in his country of origin that no child should experience, whose nervous system had been built in a context of threat, chaos, and loss.

And she was sitting across from me in a state of complete activation, unable to access any of the love she felt for him because her nervous system had filed the situation under one word: danger.

Sidney was not wrong that something needed to change. Their situation was genuinely difficult. The behavior her son was exhibiting was genuinely unsafe.

But the threat assessment her nervous system was running—the assessment that produced the words "he's going to kill me"—was not accurate. And it couldn't be accurate, because her nervous system wasn't assessing the current situation. It was assessing something else entirely, drawing on its own history, its own filing system, its own map of what danger looks and feels like.

That's what the Trainwreck of the Unconscious™ looks like in a parent-child dynamic. Not cruelty. Not failure. A nervous system doing its best with the data that was accessible.

I used the Five Questions with her. Not as a protocol—as a conversation. These five questions are designed to help a person access what their nervous system is actually responding to, rather than what it appears to be responding to. Five Questions that tap into the lower parts of the brain and bring the unconscious to awareness.

Sidney's answers changed everything. Not immediately—these things never happen immediately. But the questions created just enough space between stimulus and response for something to shift.

As we navigated the Five Questions, which I will outline below, she could see how her past was running smack dab into her current life. The stress cycles from the abuse she experienced in her past were still wide open, had not been closed, and were being activated by the filing cabinet of memory that her son was activating.

She had her own story based on her own trauma. The feelings of her traumatic past were the same feelings that were being activated by her son. They were the same feelings her son was having from his own traumatic past. It was a dance of their unconscious, on both sides, being activated in real time.

The Science

The Trainwreck of the Unconscious™ is the moment a person becomes aware that they have been living out the exact patterns from their past—their childhood, a traumatic situation, relationships they ended but never fully recovered from or processed—running in their own life right now, without their awareness. The trainwreck is a collision between who we intend to be and what we have been unconsciously doing.

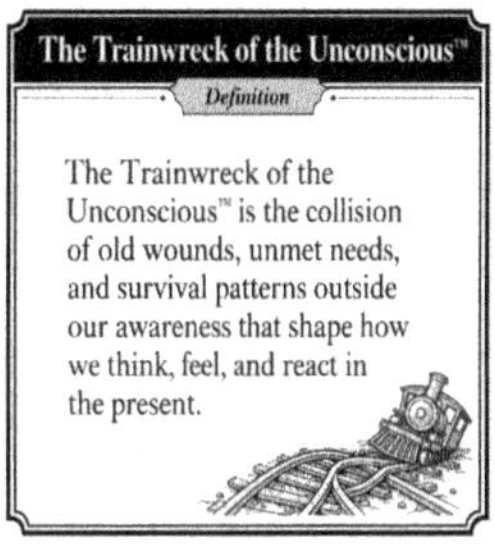

This collision can run in every setting. You can experience that crash in parenting, where a child presses on an unhealed wound the parent didn't know they still had...In workplaces, where a dynamic between colleagues activates a nervous system pattern laid down decades earlier with people who looked nothing like these colleagues but feel exactly the same... In intimate relationships, where the most ordinary interactions can suddenly carry a charge that has nothing to do with what is actually happening in the room.

The Trainwreck of the Unconscious™ is not a character flaw. It is not evidence of insufficient effort, inadequate insight, or broken willpower. It is the nervous system doing exactly what it was built to do—pattern matching at extraordinary speed, using the best available information, which is almost always older than the current moment.

The Five Questions are a tool I developed from years of clinical practice. They are designed to bring the unconscious to consciousness and assist with acknowledgement of how the past is playing out in the current moment.

The questions are designed to help someone access what their nervous system is actually responding to—beneath the surface presentation, beneath the activation, beneath the story they are telling themselves about what is happening. This framework is my original creation—developed through thousands of hours of clinical work, not adapted from any single source.

Here are the Five Questions:

One—Are my basic needs met? Am I hungry, thirsty, tired, in need of sleep, in need of movement, in need of social connection, in need of sunshine? The nervous system cannot regulate from a deficit. If any basic need is unmet, that unmet need contributes to activation in ways unrelated to the presenting situation. Address the need first. Hangry is a real thing. We know that when we are hungry, we can be more irritable. The same is true for the other basic needs.

Two—Is this person's sensory system activating mine? Are they too loud, too close, too intense? Is the environment itself—the noise, the light, the temperature, the crowding—contributing to an already stretched rubber band? Understanding this question also means understanding your window of tolerance. Everyone has a different window—a range within which the nervous system can function and process. When someone is tapping a pen, and we cannot tolerate it, this amplifies our activation.

Three—Who does this person remind me of from my past? Not consciously. Not with intention. But at the level of the brainstem, which is always pattern-matching—who does this person's voice, face, energy, or dynamic remind the nervous system of? The answer is often surprising. The colleague who activates you may remind your nervous system of a sibling. The student who drives you to the edge may remind your nervous system of a parent or a boss. Your own child may remind you of a middle school bully or a friendship you lost along the way.

Four—When have I felt this way before? What is the specific feeling that is being activated— this feeling of being out of control, of being embarrassed, of being unseen, of being dismissed, of being powerless? Many people experience this: when we attend a wake, or a funeral, or a celebration of life, we think of all the other people we have lost. This is the drawer in the filing cabinet labeled grief and once it's opened, we access all of the times we felt grief. Feelings are like that. Once we can label the feeling, or how we felt in the moment of the current activation, we can open that drawer and identify what other past experiences caused these feelings to be activated.

Five—What was I going through when I was this person's age? This question is critical when you are parenting or teaching or working with kids in another capacity. Kids have a particular way of pressing on our unhealed wounds. Not intentionally. That's just how the dance of intimacy works. When we are a safe space for children, in whatever capacity that is, that safety gives space for our wounds to be opened up. This also allows us to heal.

I don't call it resistance when a client can't access these answers immediately. I call it protection. The nervous system is protecting something. And protection is intelligent, even when it is no longer necessary.

Now I want to address something specifically about internationally adopted children, because it is relevant to the mother in this story and to the broader understanding of this framework.

Children who are adopted internationally often carry three distinct layers of trauma—and they must be understood in the order they occurred.

The first layer is preverbal. Experiences that happened before language existed. These are stored entirely in the body—in sensation, in the nervous system's most primitive filing system.

They have no narrative. They cannot be accessed through talk. They respond only to bottom-up strategies, like we discussed in Chapter 1.

The second layer occurred in a first language. Words, voices, sounds, and sensory details are encoded in a language the child may no longer regularly speak or hear. The soothing voice that once felt safe. The harsh command that once meant danger. All of it is filed in sounds the child can no longer consciously access—but the body still recognizes.

The third layer is arrival in a new country, with a new language and a new family, where they are being asked to heal from experiences that never lived in words, in a language that doesn't contain them.

When that mother began to do her own work (acknowledging her activation, closing her stress cycles)—when she began to understand what her own nervous system was carrying—something remarkable happened. She could finally see her son clearly. His activation, which had looked like danger to her nervous system, began to look like what it actually was: A child whose body held things in the language of his origin country, in the sensory memory of his earliest life.

Sidney couldn't see him before because she couldn't see past her own activation.

Once she could—everything changed.

The Skill: Acknowledge, Notice, Release

The next time you find yourself activated by someone—your child, your partner, a colleague, a stranger—I want you to try the Five Questions. Not all five at once. Not in the middle of the activation. But as soon as the scale has come down far enough for your cortex to come back online.

Sit somewhere quiet. Take a breath.

One—Are my basic needs met?

Two—Is this person's sensory system activating mine?

Three—Who does this person remind me of?

Four—When have I felt this way before?

Five—What was I going through when I was this person's age?

Write down whatever comes. One word is enough. A question mark is enough. Even noticing that your body tightened when you read question five—that tightening is information.

The questions don't resolve the activation. They acknowledge it. And located activation can be worked with in ways that unlocated activation cannot.

I also want to name something about the release part of this chapter's title.

The body must regulate—and often that means releasing something. Physiologically, not metaphorically. The nervous system has multiple pathways for discharge—crying, shaking, trembling, yawning, laughing, sighing, and even vomiting in extreme cases. These are not failures or embarrassments. They are the body completing a cycle that needs to be completed. If something wants to discharge when you use these questions, let it. You are not falling apart. You are completing something that has been waiting.

But regulation doesn't always mean releasing. Sometimes it means reorganizing, relocating, or keeping something differently. We'll talk about that more specifically in Chapters 13 and 14. For now—trust what your body needs, and don't override it in the direction of either suppression or forced release.

The Five Questions

1. Are my basic needs met?
2. Is this person's sensory system activating mine?
3. Who does this person remind me of?
4. When have I felt this way before?
5. What was I going through when I was this person's age?

From My Life

I have worked with adoptive families for more than two decades. The mother in this chapter is a composite—a single story that holds what I have seen across dozens of families in similar situations. The details are changed. The experience is real.

What I carry from that work is this: a caregiver who has done enough of their own healing to see their child clearly is the most powerful intervention available to any child's nervous system. This is not a technique nor a curriculum; this is just the creation of a regulated, present, attuned adult.

That's what the Five Questions make possible. Not perfection. Presence.

Your Journey

This journaling practice supports the practice of completing the stress cycle through:

- Acknowledging
- Noticing
- Releasing

You are not required to work with highly activating experiences. Start small. Stop anytime. Return to grounding whenever needed.

1. Acknowledge

Acknowledging means being honest with yourself about what is present.

There are no secrets here—especially from yourself. You are not judging or fixing. You are simply naming.

Use words or short phrases only.

What you are acknowledging right now:

2. Notice

Now, gently notice what is connected to what you acknowledged.

You may notice sensations, emotions, or thoughts. You do not need to analyze them.

What you notice in your body:

What you notice emotionally or mentally:

3. Ask the Body

Rather than deciding how to release, ask your body.

You may quietly ask:

"Body, what do you need right now so we can release this?"

Pause and notice.

Your body may answer right away, slowly, or not at all. All responses are normal.

What your body seems to be asking for (if anything):

4. Safe Release

If your body offered an answer, consider the safest way to honor it.

Release does not need to be intense or dramatic.

Examples include:

- Writing
- Movement
- Sound
- Art
- Tearing paper
- Lifting something heavy
- Stillness

How you chose to safely release (or plan to):

If nothing felt clear today, that's okay. Heightened awareness is enough.

5. Returning to Safety

After release—or after attempting this practice—return to safety.

You may:

- Ground through your senses
- Return to your safe space
- Feel your feet on the floor
- Take slow breaths

How you helped your body settle afterward:

6. Body Check-In
Pause and notice your body now.
You may notice:

- Neutral awareness
- Relief
- Fatigue
- Calm
- Or no change

All responses are valid.
What you notice in your body right now:

Closing Reminder
Release is not about force.
Small moments count. Stopping counts. Safety always

comes first.

Your body learns through patience, not pressure.

CHAPTER THIRTEEN

THE SHAPE, THE COLOR, THE SIZE

THE STORY

Mason was eight years old, and he had been having a hard day at school.

This was not unusual. He had a feeling, and his body acted on it. Immediately. Completely. Without the filtering system that most people take for granted, and that Mason's nervous system simply didn't have available to him in those moments.

That particular day, the school had called. Desks had been flipped. And Mason landed in my counseling office.

I had been working with his family for a while by then. We had given his parents support and resources. We had talked about how to navigate the outbursts, how to stay regulated themselves when Mason wasn't, how to communicate with the school, how to build a plan that actually accounted for what was happening in Mason's nervous system rather than just managing the aftermath of what his body had done.

But I hadn't asked Mason about what he was experiencing directly yet.

So I did.

"Mason, I want you to tune into your body for a minute. Imagine what was happening when you were flipping those desks at school. What do you notice was happening in your body?"

He thought about it. And then he said, "Miss Stacy, my body was hot."

Okay. Good. We had something.

"Was there a shape? A color? A size? A weight? A texture? A smell? Just sit with it and notice."

He sat with it. An eight-year-old boy, sitting with it. And then he looked at me and said something I have told in rooms full of people more times than I can count.

"Miss Stacy, lava runs through my body when I'm like this. Like, I literally feel like hot lava runs all through me, and I just need to get it out. The only way to get it out is to get physical—flip something or hit someone."

I want you to notice something about what Mason just said.

There are zero feelings words in that description. He didn't say he was angry, frustrated, overwhelmed, or out of control. Just lava. Hot. Running through his body. Needing to get out.

And yet—when I share this with audiences, people nod immediately. Yes. That's exactly right. That makes complete sense. Because it does. It is a 100-percent accurate description of what was occurring in Mason's nervous system. His brainstem, his sensory system, his survival response—all of it captured in a single word that an eight-year-old chose because it was the truest word available to him.

I said to him, "My friend, the problem with the lava running through your body is that it's getting all over everyone and burning them. They don't want to be around you as much. They're scared of the lava."

This was true. And Mason knew it was true. He was having a hard time with friends at school—kids his age who were, genuinely, a little scared of what happened when Mason's lava spilled.

He nodded.

"So how can we help the lava cool down—and keep it safe

while it does?"

What happened next is what happens when you give a person the right question instead of the right answer.

Mason came up with his own solutions. "I could go for a walk, or I could jump. I could take a drink of cold water. My teacher and I could have a plan for when the lava starts to boil—before it spills all over everyone."

Not a behavior plan written by adults in a conference room about a child who wasn't present. A regulation plan generated by an eight-year-old boy who finally had language for what his body had been trying to communicate all along.

We transformed his entire approach based on his words. His parents started using lava language at home. His teacher got the plan he asked for. And Mason—who had been drowning in a nervous system nobody had known how to speak to—finally had someone who spoke his language.

Because we asked what his body was noticing and we asked what his body needed. And his body answered.

I have used this exercise with clients as young as 4 and as old as 85. With educators, veterans, parents, and survivors of abuse. Every time a person is given permission to describe their internal experience in sensory rather than emotional terms, something becomes accessible that wasn't before.

A Veteran once described his anxiety to me as a rattling in his chest that feels heavy. He didn't say he was anxious, scared, or hypervigilant. He described a rattling heavy in his chest. That description told me more about where his activation lived and what it needed than any feeling words could have.

A survivor of abuse, Renee, described what happened in her body when she was triggered: fists clenched, chest tight, and triangles in her neck. Triangles in her neck. She had never been able to name what happened to her body in those moments. But triangles—that was it. That was true. And once it was true, it was workable.

This is what the exercise does. It makes the internal experience tangible. And once an experience is tangible, it is no longer running invisibly in the background. It can be looked at, described, and worked with.

Mason's lava wasn't a behavior problem. It was information. And once it had a name, it could be cooled.

The Science

This exercise is my original framework—developed over years of clinical practice, not adapted from any training. I want to be clear about that, because the shape, color, size approach emerged from thousands of hours of listening to what clients could access when feeling words were unavailable.

Smell and texture were added to this framework because a client pointed out that they were needed. She was right. Those two questions make the exercise more precise and more complete.

Here is why this exercise works—and why it works when nothing else has.

To review: We learned in Chapter 1 that the brain develops from the bottom up. The brainstem first. The sensory system and the survival responses come first. The upper parts of the brain—the part that generates feeling words, that can name and articulate and reflect on emotional experience—last. And not just last in development, but last to come online in any moment of significant activation.

When Mason was flipping desks, his cortex was largely offline. Asking him how do you feel in that state is like asking someone to describe a painting in a language they don't speak. The capacity simply isn't available. Not because Mason was unwilling, difficult, or broken. Because his nervous system was running from the bottom—from the brainstem, from the sensory system, from the survival response.

The shape, color, and size exercise works because it speaks to the lower parts of the brain. It doesn't ask for language. It doesn't require the cortex. It asks for sensation—for the body's own reporting of what it is experiencing—and the brainstem can answer that question even when the rest of the brain cannot.

Children are often better at this exercise than adults. Not because they are more emotionally sophisticated—but because their emotional centers are ripe and active during that stage of development. They say what comes up right away, without filter, because they don't know they should filter. They haven't yet built the editing function that adults spend decades reinforcing. Their bodies lead. The felt sense arrives before the cortex can redirect it.

Adults often need more time to trust their senses. Decades of being told to use feeling words, to be rational, to explain rather than describe—all of that creates distance between a person and their body's actual reporting. But this exercise is effective for adults, too. It just sometimes takes longer to trust what comes.

One more important thing. Some people cannot answer any of these questions at first. Nothing comes. The body goes quiet when asked to report.

This is not failure. This is protection. The nervous system is keeping something safe until there is enough capacity, enough safety, enough of a felt sense of being held to allow the reporting to begin. With practice, with time, with the skills being built elsewhere in this book, the answers will come. The body is always speaking. We are just learning, slowly and gently, how to hear it.

The Skill: Shape, Color, Size, Etc.

Find a comfortable position. You don't need to close your eyes.

You just need to turn your attention inward for a few minutes.

Bring to mind something that activates you. Not the hardest thing—something manageable. A situation, a person, a moment that recently produced a response in your body. This could be from your list or something on your mind today.

Now—instead of asking yourself how you feel about it, ask your body what it is noticing.

Where do you feel this experience in your body? Notice. Don't analyze. Just notice where your attention goes.

Does it have a shape? Don't force an answer. Just notice what comes. It might be a clear image. It might be a vague sense. It might be nothing at all yet—and that's fine.

Does it have a color?

Does it have a size? A weight? A texture? A smell?

Work through each quality slowly. Some will resonate. Some won't. Use what's useful. Leave the rest.

What you're building is a sensory portrait of your internal experience. Not a diagnosis. Not an interpretation. Just a description—in the most honest language available—of what is actually happening in your body right now.

Once you have something—even something vague, even a single detail—stay with it for a moment. Notice what happens when you look at it directly rather than away from it. Get a strong sensory visual of what is happening. A black hole in the stomach. A weighted orange blob in the chest. Whatever it may be, this sensory experience makes it more manageable, more tangible, easier to work with.

And then—we move to the next question. Not what does this thing need? Instead, we ask: Do I want to keep this or get rid of it?

That's Chapter 14.

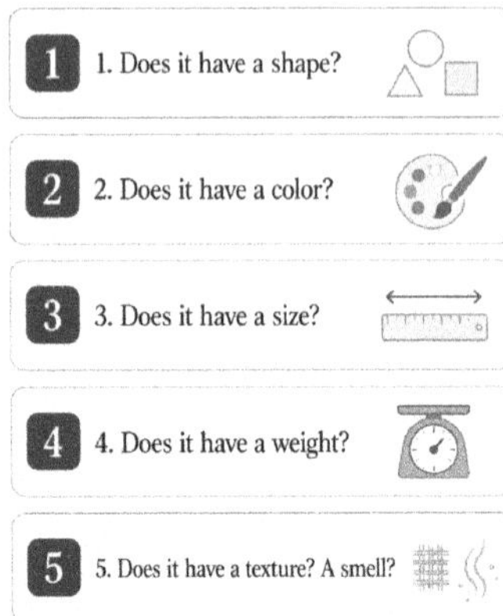

FROM MY LIFE

Mason taught me something I didn't fully know before I sat across from him.

I had been trained in various somatic and body-based approaches. I understood the neuroscience. I had used body-based questions with adults and watched them open doors that years of talk therapy hadn't been able to find.

But Mason showed me something about children that I have never forgotten.

Children are often better at this than adults because they haven't yet learned to distrust their body's language. They haven't spent years being told that feeling words are the only legitimate currency of emotional experience. They haven't accumulated years of being told, "you're being dramatic," or "that doesn't make sense," or "just calm down," that teaches a nervous system to stop reporting what it actually experiences.

Mason said lava because lava was true. He didn't edit himself. He didn't search for a more acceptable answer. He described his body's experience with complete fidelity—and in doing so, gave us everything we needed to help him.

I also want to tell you what happened to Mason over time.

He didn't stop having lava. His nervous system didn't suddenly change because we found a metaphor for his experience. What changed was that the lava had somewhere to go before it spilled. He had a plan—his plan, the one he generated himself—for what to do when he felt it starting to boil. The walk. The jump. The cold water. The signal to his teacher.

And his parents could talk about it at home. "Mason, where's the lava right now? What does it need?"

Instead of, "Mason, why did you do that? What were you thinking? Use your words."

That shift—from why to where, from words to body, from explanation to description—changed everything for that family.

It can change things for you, too.

Your Journey

This journaling practice supports the practice of:

- Sitting with an experience
- Making it tangible through visualization
- Preparing the body for safe release

You are not required to work with highly activating experiences. Start small. Pause anytime. Return to grounding whenever needed.

1. Body Scan & Noticing

Begin by settling your body. Take a few slow breaths.

Then, gently notice what is present.

What you notice in your body right now (words or short phrases):

2. Choosing One Experience

Choose one experience to work with today (a sensation, feeling, or response)

This should feel manageable, not overwhelming.

What you are choosing to notice today:

3. Making It Tangible (Choose One or Both)

You may write, draw, or do both. There is no right way to do this.

Option A: Describe It With Words

As you sit with this experience, gently ask, does it have:

- A shape?
- A color?
- A size?
- A weight?

- A texture?
- A smell?

Your descriptions:

Option B: Draw the Visual

Use the space below to draw what this experience feels like in your body.

This does not need to be "good" art. Simple shapes, lines, colors, or symbols are enough.

(This space is intentionally open.)

4. Reflection

After describing or drawing, pause and notice:
Did anything shift, soften, or change—even slightly?

You do not need to notice a change for this practice to be helpful.

5. Preparing for Release

Before release, take one slow breath.

When you're ready, you may gently ask:

"Body, what do you need so we can release this?"

You do not need an answer today.

What you notice when you ask this question (if anything):

6. Returning to Safety

After this practice, help your body settle.

You may:

- Ground through your senses
- Return to your safe space
- Feel your feet on the floor
- Take slow breaths

How you helped your body settle afterward:

Closing Reminder

You are not required to fix or change anything.

Making the experience visible makes it more manageable. Small steps count. Stopping counts. Safety always comes first.

CHAPTER FOURTEEN

Keep It or Get Rid of It

The Story

I want to tell you about Renee. She noticed triangles in her neck.

You met her briefly in Chapter 13—the survivor of abuse who described her body's experience in sensory terms when feeling words had never been available to her. Fists clenched. Chest tight. Triangles in her neck.

When we got to this question—do you want to keep it or get rid of it—she was reflective. She sat with this question for longer than I expected. I held that space with her. "It" was what her mind created...the visual, the sensation.

Renee wanted to keep them.

I want to be honest about my own reaction the first time a client chose to keep something. I had gone into this work with an assumption I didn't even know I was carrying—that the goal was always completion of the stress cycle through release. That healing meant emptying. That the measure of progress was how much had been let go.

My clients corrected me.

Because what Renee said next changed how I understood this entire process.

The triangles in her neck were connected to her survival. They were the body's record of something she had lived through—something hard and violating and real—and they were proof that she had made it. Getting rid of them felt, to her nervous system, like getting rid of the evidence. Like erasing the witness. Like losing something that, however uncomfortable, belonged to her.

So I asker her a different question.

If you're going to keep these triangles—how do you let them live in your body in a way that is safe? In a way that doesn't hurt you?

She thought about it. And then she said something I have never forgotten.

Renee wanted to move them to her shoulders. Pointing outward. Not inward, not pressing into her throat—but outward, facing the world, like protection. Like armor. Like a reminder, carried in her body, that she had survived hard things and could survivc thcm again.

So that's what we did. Together, using visualization and the body's own language, we moved the triangles from her neck to her shoulders. Where they became something different. Not a wound. A warrior's markings.

She didn't eliminate her trauma. Renee transformed it into something she could live with—something that served her rather than harmed her.

That is why we ask, "Keep it or get rid of it?" Because the body already knows the answer, and the answer is not always what we expect.

The Science

This question—keep it or get rid of it—is the one that surprises people most.

Because the logical answer, the cortex answer, is always the same. Get rid of it. Why would anyone want to keep something that causes discomfort?

But this assumes that what the body is storing is only pain, when often, what the body stores is connection—connection to a biological parent, a person we may never see again, or connection to a place where we were born and to which we can never return, or connection to a person we loved who is no longer here, or connection to a version of ourselves—younger, more vulnerable, not yet healed—who deserves to be remembered and honored rather than erased.

The body is not irrational when it holds onto these things. The body is being faithful. It is keeping the record of what mattered. And when we ask it to simply release without first understanding what it is releasing and what that release might cost—we are asking the nervous system to do something that, at the level of survival, feels like loss.

This is why the question has two equally valid answers.

Dr. Pat Ogden's work on somatic experiencing reminds us that the body's wisdom is not always legible to the thinking mind. What looks like resistance from the outside—a person who cannot release, who holds on despite wanting to let go—is often the nervous system protecting something precious. The work is not to override that protection but to understand what is being protected and find a way to honor it.

"Keep it or get rid of it" is not a test. There is no correct answer. There is only the answer that is true for this body, this experience, this person, in this moment.

Let me be equally clear about the get-rid-of-it answer, because it deserves the same attention.

Some things genuinely need to go. A pattern that is causing harm in every relationship it touches. An experience that has no redemptive thread—that was simply wrong and damaging and whose only value is in being released. A belief about yourself that was handed to you by someone who was wrong about you, and that you have been carrying far longer than it deserved.

When the body says get rid of it—that too is wisdom. And the process of physiological discharge—the shaking, the crying, the trembling, the release—is the nervous system doing what it was built to do. Completing the cycle. Filing the experience where it belongs. Making room for something new.

Neither answer is more healed than the other. Neither is evidence of more progress or less. They are simply different truths, held by different bodies, about different experiences.

Trust what your body knows.

The Skill: Keep It or Get Rid of It

After you have a visual from the shape, color, size exercise—after the experience in your body has a form, however vague—ask yourself one simple question.

Do I want to keep this or get rid of it?

Let your body answer. Not your mind. Your body.

If the answer is "get rid of it," engage your imagination in the process of release. How does your body want to let this go? Some people blow it up. Some send it down a river. Some release it into the air. Some bury it. Some burn it. The method is yours—there is no right way. Let your gut and your nervous system lead.

If the answer is "keep it," that is not failure or resistance. That is your nervous system being honest about what this thing means and what it is connected to. Ask a different question: How do we let this live safely in your body? Where does it want to go? What does it want to become?

Renee, the woman with triangles in her neck, moved them to her shoulders where they became armor instead of injury. What might your body do with what it's been holding if you gave it permission to keep it differently?

There is one more question that sometimes wants to be

asked.

What do I want to fill this space with?

If something has been released, there is sometimes a space left behind. Your nervous system may want to fill it—with safety, with warmth, with something that belongs there now. Or it may want to leave the space empty for a while. Both are valid. Let the body decide.

From My Life

I want to tell you what my clients taught me about keeping things.

I came into this work assuming that healing meant releasing. That the goal was to get as much out as possible—to empty the filing cabinet, clear the hard drive, make space for something better. I thought that keeping anything was a sign of being stuck. Of not being ready. Of having more work to do.

I was wrong.

What I have learned over 20 years is that some things deserve to be kept. Not because they don't hurt. But because they are connected to people and places and moments that mattered—that still matter—and releasing them would mean releasing the connection itself.

I have worked with adoptees who kept sensory experiences connected to their birth country. Not because those experiences were comfortable. Because they were the only thing left of a place and a beginning that was theirs before anything else was theirs.

I have worked with people who kept grief. Not the acute, overwhelming grief of early loss. But a quieter grief. A held grief. A small, warm, steady weight that reminded them their person mattered. They loved them and they carry them. That kind of grief is not a wound. It is a tribute.

I have also learned—and this took longer—that sometimes

the body says "keep it," because it is not yet ready to release. Not yet. And that "not yet," deserves the same respect as never. The body knows its own timeline.

So when the answer is "keep it," I believe it. I work with it. And I ask—how do we make this safe to carry?

Because the body is not wrong. It is only doing the best it can with what it has.

YOUR JOURNEY

You do not have to decide anything today.You are not required to let anything go.You are always in control.

This journaling practice helps you gently ask your body what it needs.

1. The Visual You Noticed

Briefly describe or sketch the visual that came up for you.

Option A: Describe it with words (short phrases are enough)

Option B: Draw it (simple shapes, lines, or colors are enough)

2. Asking the Question

Gently ask yourself:

"Do I want to keep it, or get rid of it?"

There is no right answer.

What came up when I asked this question (if anything):

3. If the Answer Is: Get Rid of It

If the answer is "get rid of it," imagine how your body would like to release it.

This is creative and personal.

Some people imagine:

- Blowing it up
- Letting it dissolve
- Sending it down a river
- Releasing it into the air

How your body wants to get rid of it (or might want to):

4. If the Answer Is: Keep It

If the answer is "keep it," that does not mean something is wrong.

Sometimes the body is saying, "Not yet."Sometimes keeping something is protective.Sometimes the body keeps things connected to people we love, grieve, or don't want to lose.

Ask your body:

"If we are going to keep this, how do we let it live in my body without hurting me—while focusing on safety?"

What your body seems to need (if anything):

5. Filling In

Whether something was released or kept, gently ask:

"What needs to fill in the space?"

This might be:

- Safety
- Warmth
- Strength
- Support
- Rest

"What does this look like?"
Describe the shape/color/size/weight/texture/smell:

What you imagine filling in (if anything):

6. Checking In
Pause and notice your body right now.
You may notice:

- Relief
- Neutral awareness
- Fatigue
- Calm
- Or no change at all

All responses are okay.
What you notice in your body now:

Closing Reminder

You do not have to finish this in one sitting. You can return to this practice at any time.

Honoring your body is the work.

CHAPTER FIFTEEN

BILATERAL MUSIC AND MOVEMENT

THE STORY

There is a school in Colorado that did something so simple and so brilliant that I think about it every time I talk about bilateral movement.

The staff put cross-body movement options outside every classroom door. They hung sheets of paper with printed instructions of each movement outside the doors.

Not inside. Outside. In the hallway.

Because here is what most schools do with dysregulated students. They send them into the hall. And here is what dysregulated students do in the hall: They chitty-chat with everyone in the hallway, they fidget, they find other dysregulated students, and they dysregulate each other further in the wrong direction. The hall becomes a collection point for nervous systems that have nowhere to go and nothing to do with what's running through them.

This school saw the science and made a different decision.

Now when a student needs to leave the classroom—when their nervous system is too activated to learn—they are sent to the hall to move. Specifically. Intentionally. Bilaterally.

They are told to do 10 jumping jacks or 15 ski jumps. These cross-body movements engage both sides of the body, cross the midline, and activate both hemispheres of the brain simultaneously. And then they are told to return to class.

They aren't punished or isolated. They're regulated and then return to the classroom.

The difference in those students when they came back through the door was measurable, and not because the jumping jacks solved whatever had activated them. The bilateral movement had done something to their nervous systems that sitting still in a chair never could—it had helped both sides of the brain talk to each other again.

I have thought about that school hallway many times since. About how much we ask of human nervous systems when we expect dysregulated people to sit still and think their way through activation. I've thought about how available this tool actually is to all of us—and about how rarely we use it.

The Science

Bilateral stimulation is not a new concept. It appears across therapeutic modalities, across cultures, across the entire span of human history. Walking is bilateral. Drumming is bilateral. Rocking is bilateral. The rhythmic, patterned, repetitive movement of the body is one of the oldest and most reliable ways the nervous system has ever found to regulate itself.

EMDR—Eye Movement Desensitization and Reprocessing, or as my colleague Ana Gomez more accurately describes it, Eyes Moving to Digest and Recover—is built on bilateral stimulation. The alternating eye movements, taps, or sounds used in EMDR sessions engage both hemispheres of the brain simultaneously. This bilateral engagement supports integration—it helps information move more smoothly between the different parts of the brain, helps the nervous system process what it has been storing, and helps the filing cabinet file the files where they need to go.

Dr. Bruce Perry's work on the Neurosequential Model identifies rhythmic, patterned, repetitive movement as one of the primary ways the brainstem regulates itself. Before the cortex can think, before the limbic system can feel, the brainstem needs rhythm. It is, at its most fundamental level, a rhythm-seeking system. And bilateral movement provides exactly that.

I want to tell you what finally sold me on bilateral music specifically.

I was trained in Brainspotting—a therapeutic modality that uses fixed eye positions to access subcortical processing, working beneath the cortex to reach what the body has been storing. During that training, I began to understand at a much deeper level why bilateral auditory stimulation—sound moving alternately between left and right—supports the same kind of deep processing that Brainspotting accesses. The music isn't background. It's an active part of the regulation process, engaging both hemispheres, creating the conditions for integration.

That training changed both my clinical and personal practice.

Bilateral stimulation comes in three primary forms, all of which are accessible for everyday use by all of us.

The first is music—specifically music with a strong bilateral quality. Bilateral music playlists are available on Spotify, Apple Music, and YouTube. The Calm app has specific bilateral music options. Or—as I used myself when I played Eminem before heading into divorce court—we can play a song whose rhythm and truth give the nervous system permission to organize itself before walking into something hard.

The second is body-based tapping. Alternating left hand, right hand. Left knee, right knee. The butterfly hug—crossing your arms over your chest and tapping your shoulders with alternating hands—is one of the most accessible bilateral practices available. Tapping can be discreetly done in a waiting room, in a car, under a desk, or anywhere a nervous system needs regulation.

The third is cross-body movement. Movements that cross the body's midline engage both hemispheres simultaneously. These include jumping jacks, ski jumps, walking, marching with opposite arm and leg movement. If you search cross-body movements for regulation, you will find hundreds of options—exercises developed for classrooms, for therapy, for athletes, for anyone whose nervous system needs both sides of the brain talking to each other.

The form matters less than the consistency. Whatever bilateral practice your nervous system responds to—use it. Use it before your activation level peaks. Use it as a daily practice, not just a crisis intervention.

The Skill: Bilateral Music and Movement

You already have two bilateral practices from earlier in this book. You just may not have named them as such.

In Chapter 9, I drove to a courthouse on one of the hardest days of my divorce and put on Eminem. The driving rhythm of that music—its bilateral quality, its alternating sounds, its relentless forward momentum—organized my nervous system before I walked into a room that required me to be present and steady. That was bilateral stimulation supporting regulation before an emotionally difficult event.

In Chapter 11, I sat on a yoga mat for ninety minutes, bilaterally tapping, while grief moved through me in waves. That was bilateral stimulation supporting regulation during release—giving the nervous system a rhythm to hold while something too big to process all at once finally found a way through.

And in a school hallway, students did jumping jacks. That was bilateral stimulation in its most accessible, most democratic, most unglamorous form. No equipment. No training. No clinical framework required.

Here is how to begin building your own bilateral practice.

Start with what you already do. Is there music that reliably changes your state? That gives your nervous system somewhere to go when activation is building? A bilateral rhythm is about left-right alternation of sound. You will notice the sounds alternating on each side. Use this intentionally.

Try the butterfly hug. Cross your arms over your chest. Place each hand on the opposite shoulder. Tap—left, right, left, right—slowly and steadily. Notice what happens in your body after 30 seconds. After a minute.

Try walking with intention. Noticing the alternation—left foot, right foot, left arm swinging forward as right foot steps. The cross-body pattern of natural human walking is bilateral. Your body already knows how to do this.

Try bilateral music. Search for it. Find a playlist that resonates. Notice how your body responds.

And if none of these feel right, search for cross-body movements for regulation. You will find hundreds of options. Try them. Let your nervous system lead.

From My Life

I want to tell you about the rocking glider.

When I became a mother, it was my number one priority. Not the crib. Not the monitor. The rocking glider.

I was studying the Neurosequential Model while I was pregnant. I was learning about my nervous system. I was aware that I was creating the sensory system of my unborn child. I knew that rocking was a regulation tool. The bilateral rhythm of it and the way it gave the body a pattern to follow when the body had lost its own helped settle the nervous system.

When my daughter was small, we rocked together in the glider. The rhythm helped both of our nervous systems find baseline in the same motion.

And here is something I learned through my training that I now teach in clinical settings: we naturally rock at our resting heart rate. That rhythm—the pace at which the body chooses to rock when it is not trying to do anything else—corresponds to the pace of a regulated nervous system. And when a child is dysregulated, a parent who rocks intentionally and slowly—deliberately bringing their own rhythm down below the child's activation—will often find that the child's heart rate follows. Co-regulation through bilateral rhythm.

Today, my adult daughter still crawls into my lap in that glider sometimes. She says, "Let's rock, mama."

And we do. Two regulated nervous systems. The same rhythm. The bilateral motion that has been part of both of our lives since before she could name it.

Your Journey

Bilateral music and movement can support regulation and integration, but it is not necessary for healing to occur.

You are always in control. You can stop at any time. Go slowly.

If you are sensitive to sound, prone to headaches, or have a history of traumatic brain injury, approach this gently or skip it altogether.

1. What You're Using Today

You may choose one, both, or neither.

☐ Bilateral music

☐ Bilateral movement (tapping, walking, cross-body movement)

☐ Neither—just noticing my body

What you chose today:

2. Setting Up for Safety

Before you begin, take a moment to set yourself up for comfort.

Volume level (if using music):

☐ Very low

☐ Low

☐ Medium

Movement type (if using movement):

☐ Gentle tapping

☐ Walking

☐ Cross-body movement

☐ Other:

3. **Body Check-In (Before)**

Pause and notice your body before starting.

What you notice in your body right now:

4. While Using Bilateral Input (Short Window)

As you listen or move, simply notice.
You may quietly ask:

- What do I notice in my body?
- Does anything shift?
- Does anything feel calmer or more activated?

There is no goal.
What you noticed during this practice:

5. Body Check-In (After)
Pause again and notice your body now.
You may notice:

- Calm
- Neutral awareness
- Fatigue
- Increased sensation
- Or no change at all

All responses are okay.
What you notice in your body now:

6. Was This Supportive?

There is no right answer.

Did this feel supportive today?

☐ Yes

☐ No

☐ Not sure

What helped or didn't help:

7. Integrating With Part 4 Skills

If helpful, note how this might support the skills you've learned:

☐ Just Notice

☐ Sit With It

☐ Visualization

☐ Keep It or Get Rid of It

How bilateral input might support your practice (optional):

Closing Reminder

You do not need to use bilateral music or movement every time.

Your body gets to decide. Small experiments are enough. Safety always comes first.

A NOTE BEFORE WE PROCEED

You did something significant in Part Four. You didn't just read about healing. You practiced it. You brought your actual nervous system into contact with these skills—imperfectly, incompletely, in whatever way was available to you. And that contact matters more than any amount of attempted cognitive understanding could.

The practices in Part Four are available as you to go back to your lists in Part Two and begin completing stress cycles. As you are ready. There is no rush. There is no timeline. You now have the resources, the tools. You also have Part Three, the support system to assist with anything that you are digesting.

Part Five is where we talk about what happens next. After the awareness has arrived, it cannot be sent back. After the work has begun to change something and after the world around you starts to shift you will notice changes in your relationships and your everyday rhythms. Part Five will help address this.

Turn the page when you're ready.

PART FIVE

Integration

You can't unknow what you know.

CHAPTER SIXTEEN

You Can't Unknow What You Know

The Story

Claire sat across from me on Zoom, my typical Zoom room office, me on one side of the screen, her on the other.

She had reached out for therapy to support her parenting. Like so many clients, this woman was committed to breaking the cycle of generational trauma in her parenting. She wanted to ensure that her children, her teens, did not experience the same parental relationship that she had endured.

Like all of my clients who come in for parenting support, Claire reflected on her own childhood journey. The relationship she had with her parents then and now. She had to notice the stress cycles that were still open from her younger self, from conversations and situations that created fractures with her parents. She invited her parents, in their current state of relationship, into repairing conversations. And, like many of my clients, her parents could not hold the pain or the repair, or the ability to provide empathy and see my client's side of the situation. Instead, Claire's parents met her with guilt, fault, and blame. Conversations that were not reciprocal. Conversations that were not safe. Conversations that were not healing or adding value to the place she was in.

This is the part of healing that is difficult. Claire could no longer unknow what she knew. This led my client to have to make a choice. Accept her parents for where they were in their journey. Choose to set boundaries and see how they react. Or, cut them off, and preserve her own health.

This is more common in the therapy room than I would like to admit. And it's deeply painful for the client.

THE SCIENCE

Here is what awareness actually does.

When we come to understand something—genuinely understand it, not just intellectually but in the body, in the nervous system, in the place where knowing becomes impossible to unknow—we cross a threshold. And crossing that threshold is permanent.

Every significant insight, every moment of genuine recognition, every time the Trainwreck of the Unconscious™ reveals itself and is truly seen—these experiences change the brain's architecture. Neural pathways are strengthened. New connections are made. The way the nervous system processes information shifts—not because we decided it would, but because awareness itself is a biological event.

You cannot decide to unknow something your nervous system has genuinely integrated. You can suppress it. You can distract yourself from it. You can choose not to act on it. But the knowing remains. And it changes the lens through which everything else is seen.

This is the stone thrown into water.

The stone doesn't ask the water's permission. It doesn't consult the other ripples or check whether the far edge of the pond is ready to be disturbed. It simply lands. And the water reorganizes itself in response—outward, in every direction, touching every shore.

Healing works the same way. When one person in a system begins to change—to see themselves more clearly, to regulate more intentionally, to set limits that didn't exist before, to respond where they used to react—the system feels it. Every relationship in that system is touched by the ripple. And each relationship responds according to its own capacity.

Some relationships can hold the change. They flex. They adjust. They grow alongside the person who is healing. And in those relationships, something extraordinary becomes possible—a depth of connection, an intimacy, an honesty to which the surface-level version of the relationship never had access.

Other relationships cannot hold these changes—not because the relationships are bad or because the people in them are bad. But because the change requires honesty that some relationships have never been built to hold.

Let me make this concrete.

Take Claire. She begins doing her own healing work—addressing the parts of her that activate, completing the cycles that have been running in the background of her parenting, building the regulation skills that nobody taught her when she was the child in the room. And slowly, something started to shift.

She is in a co-parenting dynamic with her husband. As her responses began to change—as she started to pause where she used to react, to regulate herself before she engaged, to come in with a steadiness that wasn't available to her before—his responses begin to shift, too. Not because she asked him to change. Because the system she is part of is reorganizing around her.

And the kids feel it.

Where mom used to come in with a strong tone of voice, with urgency, with the particular energy of someone who is fighting to maintain control of a situation that is already activating her—she is now regulated. Breathing. Taking a moment to observe before she responds. Tending to her own nervous system first, and then meeting her children from that more settled place.

This is not a dramatic transformation. It doesn't happen after one good day or one important conversation. It happens across hundreds of repetitions, hundreds of moments where the old response was available and the new one was chosen instead, hundreds of small recalibrations that the children feel before they can name them. The co-parenting dynamic absorbs all of this before anyone has words for what is different.

This is how systems change. Not through announcements or declarations or a single breakthrough moment. Through the accumulated weight of a person showing up differently, again and again, until the system has no choice but to reorganize around what is now true.

Gabor Maté's insight in *The Myth of Normal* is essential here. No two members of the same family experience the same family. Two children raised in the same household develop completely different nervous systems based on their temperament, their position in the family, their particular relationship with each parent, and the specific season of the family's life in which they were born. And by extension, two partners in a marriage bring two entirely different internal worlds to the same relationship. When the internal wiring is too different, the gap that opens is not anyone's fault. That gap is the consequence of two people whose nervous systems were built in entirely different conditions trying to meet in the middle of something neither fully understands about the other.

I want to say something about what happens when someone begins healing, and the people around them react.

Often—more often than anyone warns you about—the people who love you will react to your healing as though it is happening to them. You set a limit, and suddenly, you are finding yourself managing the other person's hurt feelings about the limit rather than your own experience of finally having one. This is one of the most disorienting experiences of growth. The moment you most need to be held, you find yourself doing the holding.

This is not a sign that something has gone wrong. The reactions of others signal that something real has changed. Systems react to change. And the person doing the changing often absorbs those reactions before they have any space to process their own.

The Skill: You Can't Unknow What You Know

You cannot prevent the ripple. What you can do is stay grounded in yourself while it moves.

Name what has changed in you. Not to anyone else yet—just to yourself. What do you know now that you cannot unknow? What has shifted permanently in the way you see yourself, your relationships, your patterns? Name it clearly. Give the knowing a shape so it doesn't remain a formless weight.

Notice the system's reaction without absorbing it. When the people around you react to your change, practice just noticing. This is their reaction. It belongs to them. You can hold it with compassion without taking responsibility for it.

Give relationships time before drawing conclusions. Not every relationship that struggles with your change will be lost. Some people need to see that the new version of you is still you—still loving, still present, still committed—before they can stop reacting and start engaging.

Know the difference between adjustment and impossibility. Some relationships will adjust. Others will reach a limit. Learning to recognize that difference—not prematurely, but genuinely—is one of the harder skills of integration. Your body will help you know.

And here is something I say often in sessions. Something I want you to carry:

You've been in therapy for a while now, working on this pattern in yourself. Your loved ones are just now invited to a new version of you. *Give them an opportunity to respond.*

You won't have to do this forever without limits. But you owe yourself the time to give the relationship a real opportunity before you decide what the relationship can hold.

Build toward depth. As the ripple moves outward, pay attention to the relationships that deepen rather than fracture. These are worth tending. The quality of the relationship matters more than the quantity. That is not a consolation. That is a recalibration toward what actually sustains a life.

From My Life

There was a moment when I knew.

I had asked my first husband to go to individual counseling. Not couples counseling. Because I am a therapist I know what it is to sit in the therapist's chair and on the couch as the client. I know how individual therapy opens a person in a way that couples therapy alone cannot. And I wanted him to have his own experience—not clouded by my presence, not shaped by my clinical lens, not walking into couples therapy without his own experience and support to draw from.

I wanted the playing field equalized. I didn't need him to go because something was wrong with him. I needed us both to have our own containers before we tried to work in a shared one.

His answer was direct. "These are not my problems. These are your problems. I will go to marriage counseling to support you with your issues. But I don't need counseling myself, because I am fine."

He genuinely believed that.

And in that moment, I knew something I could not unknow.

I could not stay in a marriage with a partner who could not see the dance, who could not recognize that two people in a relationship are always, inevitably, co-creating something, who assigned the difficulty entirely to one person and positioned the other as the stable one, the fine one, simply there to support the other's problems.

My knowing didn't make leaving easy. It didn't make it clean, quick, or without a devastating cost. It just made it—eventually, painfully, with years of grief trailing behind it—necessary.

A friend once said to me, "Stacy, wouldn't the world work better if we just asked each other our ACE score and then found someone with a similar number and did the healing together?"

He's not wrong.

When two people come together with very different internal wiring—different histories of activation, different nervous system baselines, different relationships to stress, vulnerability, and repair—they can love each other deeply and still find that the gap between them opens over time. They are starting with a gap in core understanding because one person knows, from the inside, what it is to live in a protective, activated state for most of childhood—and the other simply cannot access that understanding, no matter how much they want to.

As we grow and heal, the systems we built to survive stop serving anyone. And sometimes the person we built them alongside cannot grow with us.

Even as I write this, I notice heaviness in my body, a grief that has become part of me—not acute anymore, not the raw grief of the early years, but settled. Present. My grief over my divorce is a weight I carry. I have learned to carry it more lightly over time but that weight has never fully left.

My divorce is still rippling. Almost a decade later.

When we first told people, I was not prepared for what happened. The people in my life had visceral, emotional reactions. And I found myself holding space for their emotions instead of my own. I was the one going through it. And yet I was the one doing the containing, the explaining, the reassuring.

That experience taught me something I never forgot. The people who are supposed to hold space for you are not always able to—not because they don't love you, but because your change has activated something in them that they don't yet have the capacity to manage.

The ripples from that season of my life are still moving. I lost friendships. I have a more complicated relationship with my children—a complexity I hold with more care than anything else in my life, because they are the most important people in my world, and because the reorganization that divorce asks of children leaves marks that take years to understand. I hold that complexity without blame, with only the honest acknowledgment that it is the most important ongoing work of my life, and that I am still in it.

I am also more hesitant to trust than I once was. My inner circle is very small now, not because I have given up on people, but because I have gotten clear about what I need from relationships and how few people are actually in a space to offer it. Depth is a core value of mine. Reciprocity is a requirement. I want relationships where both people can be real, where honesty is met with presence rather than punishment, where the messy, the hard, and the not-yet-figured-out are held without judgment.

The world, in general, thinks I have my life together. I don't. Not always. And managing the gap between the public version of me—the clinician, the speaker, the one who holds space for everyone—and the private version—the one who still grieves, who is still feeling the ripples, who needs holding too—is its own kind of work.

What I have found, in the small circle I have built, is something I did not know was possible for most of my life.

Safety without threat.

My current husband and I have been through some of the most difficult seasons of my life together. And what I felt—what I still feel—in the moments when we are completely honest with each other, when we can be our most vulnerable and most real without any threat of backlash, when presence and empathy show up instead of punishment or withdrawal—is a safety I had never experienced before. Not in childhood. Not in my first marriage. Nowhere.

We have made mistakes. We have fractured and repaired. We have hurt each other and come back. We have done the continuous, imperfect, committed dance of two people healing alongside each other—with a deep, unconditional love for each other and for the individual processes we are both moving through.

That is what became possible on the other side of everything I lost.

That grief is real. It deserves to be named.

And so does what grows on the other side of it.

The ripple that devastated also cleared. What it left behind—the small, deep, reciprocal relationships, a new partnership built on honesty and safety, the clarity about what I need and what I will no longer accept—that is not a consolation prize. That is the life that became available when I finally stopped living for everyone else's comfort and started living in alignment with my own truth.

You can't unknow what you know.

And eventually—not immediately, not without cost, not without grief—that turns out to be a gift.

Your Journey

You do not need to complete this journaling exercise in one sitting. This is a space to notice what is becoming clearer.

1. Awareness

What are you noticing now that you may not have noticed before?

2. Relationships

A relationship that feels different as you become more aware:

3. Shifts

A shift, pattern, or realization that feels important right now:

4. Before & Now

There was a "then," and there is a "now."
What feels different between those two?

5. Choice

Where do you feel you have more choice than you did before?

Closing Reminder

Awareness is not something to fix. It is something to notice.
Take a breath. Pause here if needed.

CHAPTER SEVENTEEN

When the Pattern Outlives the Wound

The Story

Do you remember Sidney, the mother who came to me afraid her nine-year-old son was going to kill her. She was someone whose own nervous system had filed her child's activation under the same category as something much older and much more dangerous. She couldn't see her son clearly because her own activation was running too loudly to allow it.

She did her work.

She went back through her own history. She found where that activation came from—the specific, personal, deeply rooted source of what her son's big feelings were pressing on. She neutralized the activation. She completed the cycles that had been running in the background of her parenting. And she arrived at a place where she knew, consciously and genuinely, that her son would not harm her.

The wound had integrated.

And then she came to therapy and said, "Okay, Stacy. Now what?"

She looked at me across the room with the particular exhaustion of someone who has done hard work and expected to feel finished and doesn't. She said, "I know that my son will not harm me. But I am still struggling to stay in the same room as him when his feelings are so big. I still want to leave. And I am leaving. I am going to a different room when the feelings get overwhelming."

I want you to hear what this mother was describing.

She had integrated the wound. The conscious fear was gone. The clinical work around the original source of her activation had been completed. But the pattern—the leaving, the removing herself from the room, the body's instruction to get distance from big feelings—was still running. She was still reaching for the same response she had always reached for, even in the absence of the original threat.

This is not failure. I told her that clearly. This is the pattern outliving the wound.

The wound and the pattern are two separate things. Integration heals the wound. It does not automatically rewire the habit the wound built. That work is its own layer—slower, more repetitive, less dramatic than the insight work that preceded it. It requires something different than understanding. It requires practice.

So we started building her window of tolerance one small increment at a time.

Could she stay present a little bit longer before leaving the room? Not forever. Not through the full storm of her son's emotions. Just a little longer than she had yesterday.

Could she stand in the doorway? Present but not fully in the room. Close enough to stay connected. Far enough that her nervous system could manage the proximity without flooding. The doorway was a literal in-between space—not the old pattern of full retreat, not yet the new pattern of full presence. A scaffold between the two.

That's what building a new groove actually looks like. You don't have a dramatic breakthrough, a moment where everything clicks and the old pattern disappears. You can start with a doorway, a few more seconds, one small increment of something different, practiced again and again, until the nervous system learns that it can tolerate what it previously could not.

The Science

Here is something that surprises almost everyone who does this work.

You can fully integrate a wound, but the pattern it created keeps running.

Not because the integration failed. Not because there is more wound left to process. But because the wound and the pattern are two separate things requiring two separate kinds of work.

Integration addresses the past. It neutralizes the charge of a memory. It files the experience where it belongs—as something that happened, not something that is still happening. When integration is complete, the wound no longer drives the bus.

But the pattern the wound created? That lives in the nervous system's habit architecture. It was built through repetition—practiced thousands of times over years or decades, refined into something fast, automatic, and extraordinarily efficient. The nervous system doesn't abandon efficient systems just because the original threat is gone. It keeps the tool available. And under the right conditions—activation, conflict, anything that rhymes with the original wound—it reaches for that tool first.

This is not a failure of healing. This is how nervous systems work.

Dr. Bruce Perry's work on the Neurosequential Model helps us understand why. The brainstem operates through pattern recognition. It constantly scans for familiar threat signatures and responds with familiar protective measures. Speed is its priority, not accuracy. By the time the cortex has assessed whether this situation actually requires the old response, the brainstem has already initiated it.

This is why you can know, with your whole thinking brain, that your partner is not your abuser—and still reach for leaving when a conflict between you rises above a certain threshold. The cortex knows. The brainstem doesn't care what the cortex knows. It cares what the pattern says.

The good news is that the nervous system that learned one pattern can learn another. Neuroplasticity is real. New grooves can be worn alongside old ones. You can't replace the old pattern—the old groove will always be there—but you can build a new response strong enough and practiced enough that it becomes an available option.

But here is what nobody tells you about building that new groove.

You have to practice the new behavior in the moments when the old behavior is most loudly presenting itself as the only option. You cannot practice staying when there is nothing pulling you toward leaving. The practice only happens in the actual moment of pull—when the pattern is running, and you catch it, and you choose differently. Even imperfectly. Even just 30 seconds' worth of difference. Even just to the end of the block and back.

And here is something equally important that is often overlooked. We also have to practice the new skill when we are regulated—not just in moments of activation. If we only attempt the new behavior when we're dysregulated, we cannot build reliable access to it. The nervous system learns through repetition in all states. Practice when you're calm builds the muscle. Practice when you're activated uses it. You need both.

Now—a word about the different patterns.

Fight. Flight. Freeze. You've seen these three throughout

this book.

Two more deserve naming: fawn and flock.

Every one of these is a survival response. Every one was adaptive once. And every one can outlive the wound that created the pattern on which you've come to rely.

If your pattern is fight, your work is learning to pause before the heat arrives, to notice the activation before it becomes volume and urgency, to stay in the conversation without needing to win it.

If your pattern is freeze, you may find yourself going silent and unreachable when the people who love you most need you to stay present. Your work is learning that your stillness, however protective, can feel like abandonment to someone trying to reach you.

If your pattern is fawn, you may find yourself apologizing for things that weren't your fault, making yourself small in relationships that should have enough space for you to be full-sized. Your work is learning to stay in the room as yourself.

If your pattern is flock, you may find yourself unable to manage conflict without a third party, reaching for your phone before giving the relationship in front of you a chance to repair itself. Your work is learning to tolerate the discomfort of two people working something out without rescue.

None of these patterns is more healed or less healed than any other. They are all just patterns. And they all deserve the same curiosity and the same compassion.

The Skill: Creating New Patterns

The skill in this chapter is the simplest and the hardest one in the entire book.

Notice the pattern. And practice doing something different. Once. For just 30 seconds. To the end of the block and back.

Name your pattern. Is it flight? Fight? Freeze? Fawn? Flock? It may be a combination—context-specific, looking different in different relationships.

Identify your earliest signal. What does the pattern feel like in your body before it executes? Not when you're at a 10, but when you're at maybe a four or a five. Learn to recognize it earlier. The earlier you recognize it, the more space you have to choose your response.

Practice the pause. Not the resolution. Just the pause. Before the pattern executes fully, can you give yourself 30 seconds? A breath. A glass of cold water. Something that interrupts the automatic execution long enough for the cortex to come back online.

Do something different—just once. You don't have to change the whole pattern today. You just have to do something slightly different than the pattern's default. Sit in the rocking glider instead of walking out the front door. Stay in the room for five more minutes. Once. That once is the beginning of the new groove.

Have corrective experiences. Seek out safe relationships where you can practice the new behavior with someone who will not confirm your nervous system's worst fears. Find a partner who stays regulated when you can't or a therapist who models what conflict without threat looks like. These relationships are not luxuries. They are the laboratory where the new groove gets built.

From My Life

It was 4:30 in the morning. My husband and I had been in conflict—again. I don't remember the specifics, only the quality of it, only what my body was telling me to do. I got in my car. I pulled out of the driveway. The pattern executed itself with complete efficiency before I had consciously agreed to it.

I made it to the end of the block.

And then I heard my own voice, somewhere underneath the activation: *Stacy. This is crazy. You don't have to leave. You just need to breathe. You can work this out.*

I turned around.

When I pulled back into the driveway and sat in the car for a moment before going inside, I noticed what was in my chest and stomach. It took me some time to name it accurately. It was shame. I was heavy with the particular weight of having done the thing I didn't want to do—having let the pattern win, having left when leaving no longer matched the situation.

I am stubborn. Admitting I'm wrong is genuinely hard for me. Owning the impact of my choices—even choices made by my nervous system before my mind had a vote—requires something that doesn't come easily.

But I turned around. Thirty seconds into the pattern, I turned around.

And that 30 seconds—the distance between the driveway and the end of the block—is where this chapter lives.

I want to tell you what I've learned about my own pattern from my years of practicing staying instead of running.

Leaving was never about the person I was leaving. It was about what their activation triggered in my body, what it reminded my nervous system of.

Stella wasn't a threat. My husband at 4:30 in the morning wasn't a threat. But my nervous system filed certain qualities of conflict under the same category as hunting camp. And hunting camp had one available response. Leave.

The work of building a new groove has not been graceful. I still sometimes make it to the end of the block before I catch myself. I still sometimes stand upstairs wanting to leave the house before the rocking glider and the cold water bring me back. I am still stubborn. Owning my contribution to conflict is still genuinely difficult.

But I turn around more often than I used to. And I turn around sooner.

That's the measure. Not perfection. Not the absence of the old pattern. The gradually shortening journey to the end of the block.

I also want to say something about what made this practice possible for me.

I am safe now, really safe. I experience the kind of safety that comes not from the absence of conflict but from the knowledge that conflict will not result in harm. My current husband has never once used my vulnerability against me. When I have turned around and come back through the door—ashamed, stubborn, not yet ready to be fully wrong—he has been there. He doesn't punish me for leaving; he stays present for my returning.

That is what a safe relationship makes possible. Not the absence of the old pattern. The practice of a new one.

The pattern outliving the wound is not evidence that you haven't healed. It is evidence that you are human. And this layer—the behavioral layer, the groove that needs new repetitions—is simply the next one.

You've done harder things than this.

Turn around at the end of the block.

Your Journey

This journaling exercise is not about fixing the pattern. It is about noticing it sooner and practicing something different. Even once. Even for 30 seconds.

1. Naming the Pattern

Patterns are not failures. They are learned responses.

Which pattern do you notice most often?

☐ Fight

☐ Flight
☐ Freeze
☐ Fawn
☐Flock
☐ A combination

What does this pattern look like in your life?

2. The Pattern in Motion
Think of a recent moment when this pattern showed up. What happened?

What did your body tell you to do?

3. Earliest Signal
Patterns don't start at a 10. They start earlier.
What does this pattern feel like in your body at a 4 or 5?

4. The Pause

The goal is not to stop the pattern completely. The goal is to **interrupt it**.

What might a 30-second pause look like for you?
☐ A breath
☐ Cold water
☐ Sitting down
☐ Stepping outside
☐ Naming what's happening
Or something else:

5. Something Different (Just Once)

What is one small way you could do something different?
Examples:

- stay 30 seconds longer
- lower my voice
- delay leaving
- stay present instead of shutting down

Your "end of the block" moment:

6. Regulated Practice

New patterns are built when calm *and* when activated.

When you are regulated, how could you practice this new response?

7. Support & Safety
Where do you experience real safety?

Who or what helps you practice something different?

8. Reflection
What are you noticing about your pattern right now?

What feels important to remember?

Closing Reminder

The pattern continuing does not mean healing failed. It means your nervous system learned something well.

You are learning something new now.

The goal is not perfection. The goal is turning around sooner.

Take a breath. Even noticing is part of the work.

CHAPTER EIGHTEEN

THE SKILLS YOU DIDN'T GET

THE STORY

Abby came to me after a full day of professional development.

She was a teacher. She had spent the day learning about the brain, about trauma, about how early experiences shape the nervous system and how that shapes everything that happens in a classroom. We had worked through Dr. Perry's regulate, relate, reason sequence—the understanding that a child cannot learn until they feel safe, cannot connect until they are regulated, cannot access the thinking brain until the lower brain has what it needs first.

Regulate-Relate-Reason has become a mantra among many people in the education and mental health field. This is a bottom-up, trauma-sensitive approach to engaging with humans.

Abby had come in that morning with the tools she'd been given. She'd been taught to deal with troubled students with behavior plans, sticker charts, and In-School Suspension. These were the standard responses to dysregulation that schools have relied on for decades. And over the course of the day, she came to understand that none of those are bottom-up strategies, that they address the behavior without addressing the nervous system producing it—that they were not, in any meaningful clinical sense, changing anything at the root.

Abby looked at me and said, "I need help. I need more. If all the ways that we have managed behaviors are not all that effective or developmentally appropriate, I need to learn what we do instead."

That sentence—I need to learn what we do instead—is one of the most important things a person can say. It is the moment of standing at the edge of the gap and being willing to look at it directly.

I sat with her a bit longer.

We talked about relationship as the behavior change. Not relationship as a nice add-on to the real intervention. Relationship as the intervention itself. That when a child feels genuinely safe with their teacher—when they trust that this adult will not shame them, will not punish them for having a nervous system that is doing what nervous systems do—they can begin to regulate. And when they can regulate, they can learn. And when they can learn, the behavior that everyone was trying to manage with charts and systems and consequences begins, slowly and without fanfare, to shift.

Abby and I talked about how she could build a culture of regulation in her classroom. Specific, practical things. The way she entered the room in the morning. The quality of her attention when a child was struggling. The language she used when things went sideways. The difference between responding and reacting. The way repair could become a classroom norm rather than a private shame.

Abby was taking notes.

And I noticed something as she wrote—the particular focus of someone who is not just learning new information but filling in something that was missing. These were not advanced clinical concepts she was encountering. These were foundational human skills. Skills for reading a room, for staying regulated under pressure, for building trust, for repairing when something broke.

Skills she didn't get as a child. Or as an adult. Or during her education degree.

That's not a critique of her. It's a description of the gap, the same gap that runs through this entire chapter—the skills that weren't available in the environment we grew up in, that nobody taught us because nobody had been taught them either. We arrive in adulthood and in our professional lives without these skills, and we have to go looking for them on our own.

Abby was looking. That afternoon, sitting across from me with her notebook open, she was looking.

That's the beginning of filling the gap.

The Science

There is a reason this chapter exists in Part Five rather than Part One.

You had to do the mapping first. You had to see your story clearly, understand how your nervous system was built, and practice the skills that allow you to stay regulated in the presence of difficult material. Only then—from a regulated, grounded, integrated enough place—can you look at the gaps themselves with the curiosity they deserve rather than the shame they almost always attract.

Many people grow up in homes where a full range of emotions is not welcomed, invited, or safe.

Not because their parents were monsters. But because their parents grew up in the same kind of home. And their parents before them. And somewhere back in the line—maybe on a ship in the Pacific, maybe in a different kind of crisis entirely—something happened that couldn't be processed. That got filed incompletely. That passed forward.

Through thousands of subtle cues and interactions—a parent who leaves the room when feelings get big, a family that changes the subject when something hard surfaces, a household where the unspoken rule is we don't talk about that—children learn to manage their emotional experience rather than move through it. They learn to suppress rather than express, to comply rather than stay curious, and to keep things internal rather than bring them into the relationship.

This is the difference between a home organized around compliance and a home organized around curiosity.

A compliance-based home teaches children that their internal experience is a problem to be managed. Children learn that big feelings are inconvenient, that the right response to difficulty is to get it under control as quickly as possible and return to the surface. Children in these homes become extraordinarily good at appearing fine. They learn to read the room, to manage their presentation, to perform okayness when they are not okay. These are survival skills. And they come at a cost.

A curiosity-based home teaches children that their internal experience is information worth exploring, that big feelings are allowed to take up space, and that the honest response to difficulty is to stay present with it, to name it, to bring it into connection rather than manage it alone.

Most homes fall somewhere on the spectrum between these two. And many parents who created compliance-based homes were doing the very best they could with what they had been given.

But the gaps are real. And they surface—reliably, specifically, and often painfully—in three particular contexts.

The gaps show up first in relationships. We don't know what we didn't get until we encounter someone who does it differently. We may spot these gaps through a first love who apologizes and means it, or a friend who can be angry but stay present, or a partner who can hold conflict without inflicting punishment or withdrawing. These encounters are often the first moment a person realizes, "Oh! There is another way.

Which means I didn't know what I was missing."

The second place we experience these gaps is the workplace. Professional environments surface skill gaps in high definition when we cannot receive feedback without shutting down, or when we over-apologize and over-accommodate because asking for what we need feels dangerous. Or when a coworker does these things. The workplace doesn't care about your history. It just reveals your patterns.

The third place where the gaps blindside us is parenting. And this is the one I want to stay with, because behind closed doors—in therapy rooms, in the work I do every day—this is where the gaps show up most consistently and most painfully.

I have spent hundreds of hours talking with parents about the literal brain development that toddlers go through. The tantrums. The word no. The enormous emotional expressions that seem disproportionate to every situation because the cortex isn't online yet, and the body is just doing what bodies do. These are normal. They are developmental.

And they activate parents in ways that have nothing to do with the child.

The parent who was never allowed to have big feelings often cannot tolerate their child's big feelings—not because they are bad parents, but because their child's healthy developmental expression is pressing on an unfinished part of their own nervous system. An incomplete stress cycle from their own childhood is still running, still looking for completion.

Now—a brief word about two concepts that belong in any honest conversation about how gaps get filled.

Transference is the unconscious redirection of feelings from a past relationship onto someone in the present. For example, a client may begin to experience their therapist as a parental figure. This is not pathology. It is the nervous system doing what nervous systems do—using present relationships to process what was unfinished in past ones.

Countertransference is the therapist's side of that equation—the therapist's own unconscious emotional responses to the client, shaped by the therapist's own history and unfinished business. For example, a client reminds the therapist of his big brother, who was always critical of him, causing the therapist to feel irritated or defensive around their client.

Both are real. Both are powerful. And both extend far beyond the therapy room. This dance between transference and countertransference happens in classrooms, in parenting, in friendships, marriages, and workplaces. Anywhere that a present relationship activates something from a past one.

The Skill: Learning New Skills

Before we talk about filling in the gaps, we have to name them.

This is harder than it sounds. Because gaps, by definition, are absences. And absences are often invisible.

Here are some questions to sit with:

In your relationships, what do you find most difficult? Conflict? Repair? Receiving care? Asking for what you need? Trusting that someone will stay?

In your work life, what patterns show up that feel bigger than the situation? Where do you shrink when you shouldn't?

In your parenting, or in your relationship with children generally, what behaviors activate you beyond what seems proportionate? What does your child do that quickly sends you somewhere old and dark?

Once you can name a gap, you can begin to fill it. And here is what I have learned about how that filling the gap actually happens.

It almost never happens the way we plan.

Corrective experiences—the relational moments that give us what we didn't get, that show us a different way is possible—often arrive unexpectedly in places we didn't think to look. For me, I didn't expect to find corrective experiences around male relationships in the Army. Yet, there they were. Every interaction gives us data about what we didn't get, what we need to learn, or what we are doing well. That is not an accident. That is the nervous system seeking what it needs, finding it in the available relationships, and using it—often without our conscious awareness—to fill in what was missing.

You don't have to manufacture corrective experiences. But you can stay open to them. You can notice when a relationship is offering you something you didn't have before. You can choose to receive it rather than deflect it.

And you can practice the new skill when you're regulated—not just in the moments of activation. The more familiar your nervous system is with the experience of receiving something new and surviving it, the more accessible that capacity becomes when activation is high.

From My Life

I have been thinking about my grandfather for most of my adult life.

We called him Grandpa Chuck. He served in the United States Navy during World War II and was aboard the USS St. Lo—a ship that was struck by a Kamikaze pilot in October of 1944. He watched several of his battle buddies die at sea. He was one of the few who survived.

He came home from that war and never spoke of it.

What he brought home instead lived in the body—the way it always does when there are no words, no container, and no one to witness what happened. He collected things. Coins, gold, everything he could get his hands on. After he retired from the post office, he would sit outside his house in his Bronco for hours. Sometimes days. This was a typical PTSD response. No rhyme or reason as to why, just something his body told him to do. Like he was frozen, still floating in the water, except sitting in his truck. When we visited him as children, his house was what we would call a hoarder's home today. He was always kind and always had a story to tell. But the story he never told—the one that shaped everything—was the one from the war.

As I became a therapist, I understood what I was seeing. Grandpa Chuck had come home from World War II with shell shock that was undiagnosed and never treated. What we now call Post-Traumatic Stress Disorder was living silently in this man who had no language for it and no tools to complete what had been started on that ship.

That shell shock shaped how he parented my father. We heard stories of Grandpa pulling a picket off the fence and spanking all the kids for how they acted when he was away for work. How my father was parented shaped how my father parented me. And the skills that couldn't be passed down—because you cannot give what you don't have, because you cannot teach what was never modeled for you—those gaps moved forward through the generations as faithfully as any inheritance.

I didn't fully understand the breadth of this until a few years ago, when I drove two hours across rural Colorado into rural Wyoming to sit at my father's table and ask to see Grandpa Chuck's military records. My daughter Stella came with me. We had lunch. We visited about superficial things. And then my father pulled up YouTube.

The three of us—my father, my daughter, and I—watched a 58-second video together. A Kamikaze pilot hits the USS St. Lo. This was the moment that had defined my grandfather's life. The beginning of a thread that ran through my father's childhood, through my childhood, through an ACE score of 7, through a divorce, through a deployment, through 20,000 one-on-one conversations, and this book.

I'll tell you that full story in the conclusion of this book.

What I want to name here is simply this—the skills Grandpa Chuck didn't get from a war-torn nervous system that never healed became the skills my father didn't get. And the skills my father didn't get became the gaps I spent decades trying to fill. This didn't happen because anyone was specifically intentional or because anyone chose to withhold a specific skillset. This happened because incomplete stress cycles pass down to the next generation—because the nervous system can only give what it has received.

This is not blame. This is the dotted lines of generational transmission becoming visible. And once you can see them—once the dots connect into solid lines—everything changes.

The gaps that have been most present in my own life are relational. Specifically, I did not know what healthy relationships with men looked like for a very long time. I grew up with a father whose violence was unpredictable, whose drinking removed him from himself, whose capacity for genuine connection was limited by everything he was carrying from the generation before him.

And then I joined the Army National Guard at 35.

I have thought many times about why a woman my age, with my history, ended up in uniform. Clearly there was a deep, unmet need at play, a pull toward something I didn't fully understand—toward the institution that Grandpa Chuck had served, toward an environment where I would encounter men I had never encountered before.

The particular men in my Army circle were men that offered me corrective experience. While not all Army men are like this, T\these men were protective without being abusive. They showed a full range of emotion without feeling inadequate. They listened and partnered to solve problems. They showed up for each other in ways that my nervous system had no template for.

I didn't know those men existed. Not because I was naive, but because my developmental environment had never shown them to me. The military did. And something in my nervous system, slowly and without fanfare, began to update its skills.

That is a corrective relational experience. Not therapeutic. Not planned. Just life filling in what childhood couldn't provide, when the nervous system was finally ready to receive it.

Early in my career—in my first years of private practice, working primarily with children and families—something was happening that I didn't fully understand until much later.

On some unconscious level, my clients were filling in gaps for me.

I wasn't making my clients responsible for my healing. I want to be clear about that. The ethical boundary between a clinician's needs and a client's care is absolute, and I have never crossed it consciously. But the unconscious doesn't ask permission. What I have come to understand, looking back, is that working with children—knowing what an ACE score of 7 means a child needs, knowing what attunement, protection, and repair feel like in a child's nervous system—allowed the child parts of little Stacy to receive something through the act of giving.

I could give children what I had needed. And in giving it, something in me learned what it felt like to receive.

This is transference and countertransference at their most human. This projecting and receiving happens in classrooms, too—many educators enter teaching to give students what they never got. It happens in parenting. It happens in friendships, mentorships, and communities of every kind.

I am not ashamed of this. I think it needs to be named. Because if we pretend that clinicians and educators and parents are purely givers—unaffected, untouched by the people they serve—we are lying about what it means to be human in relationship.

Every interaction teaches us something about ourselves that we need to know or didn't get.

That is not a flaw in the system. That is the system working exactly as it was designed to.

Your Journey

This journaling exercise is about noticing—not judging. You are allowed to learn skills at any point in your life.

1. Awareness
A skill you realize you didn't get:

2. Impact
How has not having this skill shown up in your life?

3. Curiosity
What might it look like to begin learning this skill now?

4. Support
One place to build this skill:

Closing
There is no failure in learning later. There is only growth.

CHAPTER NINETEEN

HEALING AT DIFFERENT PACES

THE STORY

Daniel was referred to me by another client. That's how they often get to me. A friend says, "Have you tried therapy? No? Here's a number to my therapist. Give her a call."

He called and we scheduled.

When I asked Daniel what was happening, he explained the dynamic between him and his wife. He had been doing a lot of growing and changing and self-awareness work for quite some time. His changes had created a ripple effect that was now unmanageable. He and his wife were constantly at odds—tension, arguing, the kids feeling all of it. She was not interested in individual therapy or couples counseling.

He came alone. And we started the work.

We began by lowering his activation. We started closing stress cycles. We were neutralizing the strong responses that had been running on an old pattern. And as his regulation became more solid, something else came into focus—the gap between where he was and where his wife was had become impossible to ignore.

He began to notice something in their conflicts. He was showing up differently. When tension built, he was more regulated—present, ready to work things out, using the skills he had been building. She was continuing to argue the way they always had. Escalating. Yelling. Running the same patterns he was actively trying to break. He could feel himself holding steady while the old dynamic kept reaching for him, and he could feel how alone he was in trying to make these changes.

That's one of the loneliest experiences in a relationship. Being the one who has changed. Being the one standing in the new place, looking back across the gap, realizing the other person is not yet moving toward you—and may not be interested in coming with you.

As the shifts in him became more solid and grounded, he could feel the weight of what he was coming to understand. The sadness of two decades of living with someone who wasn't interested in growing and the recognition that his marriage was not going to work out was catching up with him.

I want to pause here and name something. It is not always like this. Some people, when they see their partner doing the healing work, get curious. They get interested. Maybe they step onto the path a little further back, but still moving in the same direction. Some relationships grow into something deeper and more honest because one person had the courage to start. That is real, and it happens, and it is worth hoping for.

This was not that situation.

In this situation, the marriage ended. Daniel and his wife agreed to part ways. They agreed together that the gap between them had become too wide, and that it was no longer in the best interest of their children to live inside a wave of ripples that never seemed to settle.

He came to a therapy session after that decision had been made, still sitting with the weight of it. And I said to him what I believe to be true—what I have said to others in similar situations, and what I want to say to you now if you are living through something that feels like this story.

"Healing goes at different paces. Only you, in your heart,

know what you need and how to stabilize yourself. You've worked hard to break generational patterns, and you need to listen to that. That's hard work. That's the gift you are passing onto your kids. Using your voice, regulating a home—those are important."

That is not just consolation. That is the truth.

The work you have done—the cycles you have completed, the patterns you have interrupted, the new grooves you have worn through hundreds of small repetitions—that does not disappear because a relationship could not hold it. It lives in you. It lives in how you show up for your children. It lives in the home you regulate and the voice you use and the repair you offer when you miss.

The gap between two people healing at different paces is real, and it is painful, and sometimes it ends things that mattered.

And the healing was still worth doing.

The Science

When one person in a system begins to heal, the system feels it.

You already know this from Chapter 16—the stone in the water, the ripples reaching every relationship. What we didn't fully explore there is the range of responses that ripple can produce.

Some relationships flex. When you change, the people in those relationships find a way to adjust—not easily, not without discomfort, but genuinely. These relationships often deepen in ways that weren't possible before.

Some relationships cannot handle change. Not because the people in them are bad or unloving, but because the change requires something of both people—a willingness to look, to acknowledge, to grow alongside—for which not everyone is ready.

And I want to say something here that most books on healing don't say clearly enough.

Some relationships need to be ended. Not just held at a distance. Ended.

When abuse is ongoing. When harm is continuous and unacknowledged. When children have spent the majority of their lives over-functioning due to a parent's emotional needs—carrying the parent's feelings, managing the parent's reactions, shrinking themselves to keep the parent stable—and when that adult child finally asks for some equal footing, some reciprocity, and it simply isn't there and won't be there, more than distance may be required.

No one should be required to maintain a relationship that causes ongoing harm simply because the other person is family. The guilt-tripping, the refusal to take any ownership, the sneaky behavior, the absence of genuine reciprocity—these are legitimate reasons to step fully back from a relationship, not just to manage your expectations of it. Your healing does not obligate you to accept ongoing harm from the people who caused the original wound.

And then there is an experience I encounter constantly in therapy rooms but rarely see discussed clearly.

The adult child who has done this work—who has developed the capacity for emotional regulation, honest communication, sitting with discomfort, and staying present in conflict—sometimes finds that they have grown beyond what their parents can offer relationally.

Not in love. Love is often not the issue. But in the specific skills that make a deep, honest, mutual relationship possible.

The parent who is still living in compliance-based patterns. Who changes the subject when things get hard. Who cannot hear feedback without becoming defensive. Who meets your honesty with denial or minimizing. This parent is not maliciously withholding connection. They are operating from the limits of what their own nervous system has learned. And recognizing that—naming it clearly, without blame, with compassion for both people—is often one of the most liberating and most painful moments in a healing journey.

Lindsay Gibson's work in *Adult Children of Emotionally Immature Parents* names this dynamic with precision and compassion. Once you see it, you cannot unsee it. And the grief that follows—the grief of wanting a parent who can meet you and recognizing that your parent cannot, at least not yet—that grief deserves space. The grief of realizing you will never have the parent you deserved is a trauma. That stress cycle ought to be completed, not bypassed.

Dr. Bruce Perry's framework helps us understand the nervous system piece. We cannot access emotional depth—genuine empathy, honest vulnerability, the capacity to stay present with someone else's pain—from a dysregulated state. A parent whose nervous system is still operating primarily in protection mode cannot offer their child the attunement that the child needs, regardless of how much they love them.

Which brings us back to what makes repair possible when it does happen.

Repair requires two things. Time—enough of it for both people to develop what they need to bring to the table. And continued presence in the relationship—the willingness to keep showing up, to not give up on the possibility of something deeper.

My mother and I had both. Decades of individual living and surviving and accumulating enough life experience that when we finally sat down to talk about hunting camp, we were both standing in different places than we had been when it happened.

You cannot force that. You cannot manufacture it. But you can stay in the relationship while it develops. And sometimes—not always, but sometimes—the other person walks through therapy door, too.

The Skill: Holding Two Truths

The skill in this chapter is one of the most nuanced in the entire book. It requires holding two things simultaneously that feel like contradictions. First you need to protect yourself, and second you need to try to stay in the relationship when it is possible for you to do so without harming yourself.

Here is what I have learned about navigating the complicated relationships with people who love you and also hurt you, whose capacity is limited but whose love is real.

To make this work, you need to adjust your expectations without abandoning the relationship—so long as it's safe to continue. If your parent cannot offer depth, stop expecting depth from them, and find depth elsewhere. Let them offer what they can—presence, consistency, love in its simpler expressions—without requiring more than they have available. This is not settling. This is you adjusting your perception of what the relationship is and can be in this season.

Protect your healing without performing it. You do not owe anyone a front-row seat to your growth. Share what you choose to share. Hold the rest.

Give people time before reaching conclusions. You've been working on this for however long. The people around you are just now being invited to a new version of you. Give them an opportunity to respond before you decide what the relationship can hold.

Name exactly what you need, clearly and simply. Not as a demand. But honestly. This is what I need from this relationship right now. This is what I can offer. This is what I am no longer able to do.

Grieve what the relationship cannot offer. Do your grieving

in the appropriate containers—therapy, trusted relationships, your own internal work. The grief of wanting more from a relationship than it can currently give is real. The trauma of that loss deserves completion.

And stay open to what is possible later—when that is appropriate and safe. People change. A relationship that cannot hold you today may develop capacity in time. Keeping the door open—even from a distance, even with limits firmly in place—honors the possibility of what could be without requiring you to live in what isn't yet.

From My Life

My mother and I have divorce in common.

That sounds like a simple statement. It is not. In our family of origin, divorce had never happened. Not in her generation. Not in her parents' generation. The expectation—spoken and unspoken, cultural and familial—was that you stayed. Whatever the cost. However great the distance between who you had become and who you needed to be.

When my marriage of 18 years ended, my mother was one of the few people in my life who understood something essential about what I was moving through. Not because she had the clinical language. Not because she had done the therapeutic work that I had done. But because she had her own version of the same story. She'd been married for 28 years. She'd demonstrated the particular courage of leaving a relationship she'd been in all her adult life. She'd carried the grief that doesn't announce itself as grief because there is always something practical that needs doing.

That shared experience—two women from a family that had never navigated divorce, both navigating it—cracked open a door between us that had never opened before.

We began to talk, not about the surface things, but about

the habits our marriages had created and the dynamics we had each lived inside. We talked about how we had each survived. We shared what it was like to live in marriages where we didn't speak up, where we just complied, where we sacrificed ourselves for the sake of our children. And somewhere in those conversations—gradually, without a single defining moment, the way most real repair happens—we talked about hunting camp.

My mother also went to therapy. I want to name that because it matters. The capacity to repair is not just a function of time. It is a function of the work each person is willing to do. My mother did her work. And the conversations we had—about our marriages, about our families, about that day at hunting camp—were only possible because her own healing created the capacity for these conversations, without blame or excuses.

My mother was able to offer me something I had waited a long time to receive: An authentic, sincere apology.

She didn't offer me a defensive explanation or a minimizing reframe. She gave me a real apology. By then, she was a woman who understood what it meant to be in survival mode and who could look back with compassion and accountability at the person she had been on that day—the woman who drove her daughter back to camp and asked her to apologize—and see her clearly.

And I was able to receive her apology. Not because I had decided to extend something before I was ready. By then, I had done enough of my own work to understand that she had been in her own survival mode and had been protecting herself the only way available to her at the time.

That understanding—hard-won, arrived at slowly, built from years of therapy and corrective experiences that allowed me to close my own stress cycles—is the difference between genuine compassion and performing compassion before it's ready to arrive. You cannot rush to compassion. You have to close your own stress cycles first. And then, sometimes, the compassion arrives on its own.

My mother today is one of the most supportive people in my life. She shows up for me in the big moments and the ordinary ones. She has been present for my hardest seasons—when I became a mother, when I went through my divorce, and while I've been navigating the complex terrain of parenting my own children. When I have struggled as a parent, she and I have talked about how complicated and layered the experience is. She champions her daughters. She is proud of us. She wants the best for us.

We still have the particular tension that mothers and daughters hold toward each other. But she is my friend. I respect her place in my life. I respect her life.

There was no single conversation that changed everything between us. No breakthrough moment. Instead, there was time, shared experiences, and the willingness—on both sides—to keep showing up for the relationship through all of its seasons. The ups and the downs. The tender places and the easier ones.

Repair happened because we continued to be in relationship with all its ups and downs. We never gave up.

That's it. That's the whole secret. And it is both simpler and harder than anyone tells you.

I want to name something about my mother's repair that I think is important.

The apology she offered me was possible because of what she had been through and because of the work she did. Not because time alone heals all things—it doesn't. But because time, combined with her own willingness to go to therapy, to look honestly at her own life and her own patterns, gave her access to something she hadn't had before. She could see me more clearly. She could see what I had been inside of at 16. She could acknowledge the harm that she did to me that day. She could see her own patterns of abuse. And she could finally say what needed to be said.

I also want to mention what I had to do before I could receive that apology.

I had to close enough of my own stress cycles first.

This is the part that no one tells you about repair: You cannot receive what you haven't yet created space for. That genuine compassion—not performed compassion, not the version you offer before it's ready because you think you should—requires that your own nervous system has processed enough of its own activation to have room for something new.

Human beings are not all good or all bad. We are mixed. We have depth. Compassion comes from seeing that depth.

But we cannot often get to that compassion without first closing our own stress cycles around the harm.

That is the sequence. That is the work. And it cannot be rushed—not for our sake, and not for the sake of the people with whom we are trying to repair.

My mother and I are still in a relationship while still navigating the particular tension that mothers and daughters hold. We are still showing up for each other in the ways we can. She is one of my people. She is not a perfect person—no one is—but she's someone who kept showing up for me, who offered what she could, and who was willing, when the time came, to say the apology I needed to hear.

That is enough. More than enough. It is, in fact, everything.

Your Journey

This journaling exercise is a space to gently notice shifts in relationships. There is no need to resolve anything here.

1. Relationships

A relationship that feels different as you heal:

2. Body Awareness

What do you notice in your body when you think about this relationship?

3. Pace

Where might you be healing at a different pace than someone else?

What does your body feel when you think about that gap?

4. Boundaries & Compassion

What is one way you can:

- honor your healing

- and remain grounded in this relationship

Closing Reminder

A change in relationships does not mean something is wrong. It often means something is shifting.

CHAPTER TWENTY

Parenting and the Ripple Effect

The Story

When I became a single mother, I quickly realized that my parenting role was no longer going to be primarily about curfews, bedtimes, and rules.

We divorced. We shared custody. We navigated parallel parenting—and for those who have been through it, you already know what that word carries. The constant recalibration. The holidays split in two. The custody switches. The particular exhaustion of parenting in two separate households with two separate rhythms, across a divide that no one chose, and everyone is learning to navigate against their will.

In that season, I made a decision.

A crisis arose during what should have been an ordinary moment—a limit I set around a cell phone that became much bigger than the situation warranted. The activation in the room was enormous. Way too big for a phone. And I recognized, in the middle of it, that I was standing at a crossroads that had nothing to do with screen time.

I could die on this hill. I could enforce the limit, hold the line, be the consistent parent that culture told me children need. I could win the argument—but lose something I couldn't afford to lose.

Or I could recognize what was actually happening: My children were living through an upheaval that had reorganized their entire world, and the activation in the room wasn't about the phone.

The hill worth dying on was the relationship.

Not the curfew. Not the cell phone. Not the rules that other parents were focused on in their intact households with their predictable routines. In this season, with these children, navigating this specific upheaval, our relationship would have to provide the structure they needed. Showing up emotionally would have to provide the consistency. Connection was the rule worth keeping when I had to let go of everything else. .

I let a lot of things go in those years. Things that felt important. Boundaries that, in a different season, I would have held firmly. I held them loosely because I understood—through my own work, through more than 20 years of sitting with families in crisis, through everything this book has been building toward—that the nervous system needs safety before it can learn. Most importantly, I understood that relationship is not one tool among many; it is the foundation on which every other tool rests.

I recognized I was parenting individuals with individual needs in individual circumstances that shifted constantly and required constant recalibration.

And slowly—not linearly, not without cost, not without the particular grief of watching your children navigate something you wish they didn't have to—something held. I realized that I was breaking cycles of trauma, a lack of skills that was passed on to me.

The Science

I want to say something that might surprise you.

Toddlers are the most emotionally healthy people in most rooms.

Stay with me.

A toddler has a feeling. Their body feels it completely and immediately—there is no gap between the emotion and its physical experience. They express their feelings fully, without apology or concern for whether it is convenient. They release it—the cycle completes, the activation discharges, the nervous system returns to baseline. And then they move on. Ready for the next moment. Unburdened by what just passed. Ready to be your best friend again. Even if you are still reeling from the upheaval of that emotional and physical expression.

Children naturally know how to complete the stress cycle. They do it instinctively because their cortex isn't fully developed yet—which means the editing function, the suppression mechanism, the learned capacity to bypass the emotional experience and skip straight to managing it—none of that is fully online yet. Their bodies lead. Their feelings move through them the way feelings are designed to move.

What happens over time—through thousands of interactions in homes that prioritize compliance over curiosity, through messages like "stop crying" and "you're fine" and "that's not a big deal"—is that children learn to interrupt the cycle. To take the off-ramp. To manage their emotional experience rather than complete it.

By the time most people reach adulthood, the natural, emotional capacity they had as toddlers has been substantially overridden by years of learned suppression. And the work of healing—the work of this entire book—is, in many ways, the work of returning to what the toddler already knew how to do:

Feel one's feelings, express them safely, let the cycle of stress complete, and move on.

This is why parenting is such a powerful context for healing—and such a powerful trigger for what hasn't healed.

The parent who was never allowed to have big feelings often cannot tolerate their child's big feelings. Not because they are bad parents, but because their child's healthy developmental expression is pressing on an unfinished part of their own nervous system.

This is the ripple effect of unhealed experience on parenting. And it runs in both directions.

Your healing changes how you parent. And your children—in their natural, unedited, toddler-honest way—teach you about your own nervous system in a way nothing else could.

Now I want to talk about the parents for whom a typical parenting journey simply is not available. Not because they are failing—but because the children they are raising require something that standard parenting frameworks were never designed to address.

I have worked with internationally adopted children and their families for more than 20 years. I've helped more than a hundred children and their families. And what I have learned in that work has shaped everything I understand about what parenting actually requires.

These children carry trauma that is complex in ways that most people—including most clinicians—don't fully appreciate.

The sequence of what they experienced matters. And it must be understood in order.

First—preverbal trauma. Experiences that happened before language existed. These are stored entirely in the body—in sensation, in the nervous system's most primitive filing system. They have no narrative. They have no words. They respond only to bottom-up strategies that focus on soothing the autonomic nervous system, rather than appealing to logic or reason

Second—trauma that occurred in a first language. Words, voices, sounds, and sensory experiences that carry activation in a language the child may no longer regularly speak or hear. All of it encoded in sounds the child can no longer consciously access—but that the body still recognizes.

Third—arrival in the United States. A new language. A new family. A new sensory environment. And now—in many cases—being asked to heal from experiences that they never understood in words, in a language that doesn't contain them.

"Tell me how you feel" doesn't work with these children. Not because they are unwilling, but because the experience doesn't live in language. It lives in the sound of Velcro—the same Velcro that strapped a small child into a seat during something terrifying, now activating that child's nervous system in a classroom a decade later when a backpack opens. It lives in the particular quality of a crowded space. In a smell. In a texture. In any sensory detail that the nervous system filed under "this is what danger feels like" before the child had words for danger.

I have worked with children who experienced hurricanes in the backs of vans before they had the language to understand what a hurricane was. I have worked with children who were exposed to sexual violence in their countries of origin—experiences that the body holds in ways that no amount of talking will reach. I have worked with children whose earliest experiences were so overwhelming that their nervous systems built protection systems so efficient that they could function in the world while remaining completely unreachable through conventional therapeutic or parenting approaches.

For these children—and for their parents—bottom-up strategies are not a supplement to normal parenting. Addressing the physiological and sensory aspects of psychological distress is the only path available.

And what I have found, consistently, across more than a hundred children and their families, is this: the single most important factor in a child's healing is a caregiver who has done enough of their own work to stop reacting and start seeing.

When a caregiver can distinguish between their own activation and their child's—when they can notice that what they are feeling in response to their child's behavior is partly about the child and partly about their own history—the quality of the relationship shifts. The caregiver can stay regulated when the child is not. **And a regulated caregiver, present and not flooded, is the most powerful co-regulation tool available to any child's nervous system.**

So while parents of the internationally adopted may face extra challenges, there really is no ordinary parenting. There never was.

The best parents are parenting individuals—with individual needs, individual histories, individual nervous systems that require individual approaches. Parenting is not a formula. It is a relationship. And like all relationships, it requires the capacity to see the actual person in front of you—not the child you expected, not the child that parenting books describe, but this child. In this moment. With this history. Needing this specific thing.

That capacity to see—to truly see—is what your own healing makes possible.

The Skill: Parenting the Individual

Healing changes parenting. Not all at once. Not in a straight line. But in specific and observable ways that your children will feel before you can articulate them.

You begin to distinguish between your activation and your child's. You notice that what you are feeling in response to their behavior is not only about their behavior. And you begin to address yourself before you respond to them.

This is the most important parenting skill this book can offer. Not a technique. Not a script. Just tend to your own nervous system first. Regulate yourself before you try to regulate them—because you cannot co-regulate a child from a dysregulated state.

Once you have worked on your own triggers, closed your stress cycles from your past, and lowered your activation, you can begin to let the hill worth dying on be the relationship. You will be less likely to take on every battle or fight back on every limit. You will begin focusing on the connection and the knowledge that in your child's nervous system you are safe and present and will not abandon them emotionally, even when you are setting a limit or holding a boundary.

You will also find yourself more able to repair relationship fractures when you make a mistake. And you will make mistakes. Every parent does. The fractures are not the measure. The repair is. A child whose parent repairs consistently learns something essential—that relationships can break and be mended.

When you have seen what your own nervous system needs, you will begin to see your child. Not their behavior—the child underneath the behavior. The activation that is running. The stress cycle that needs completing.

And for those of you parenting children who carry complex histories, the skill is even simpler and even harder.

Stay regulated. Stay present. Stay curious about what the body is saying when words are not available.

The rest will follow.

From My Life

I have learned more about parenting from my clients than from any book or training.

I have sat with internationally adopted children whose bodies held things their minds could not access. I have watched bottom-up strategies reach places that years of talk therapy couldn't touch. I have seen a child's nervous system begin to soften—not because they understood what had happened to them, but because someone finally stopped asking them to explain it and started asking their body what it needed instead.

I have also sat with the parents of those children, parents who came in exhausted and confused and heartbroken. They had done everything right by every conventional parenting standard and still found themselves with a child whose behavior made no sense.

And what I have seen, in those families, is that the turning point almost never comes from a new parenting strategy. The breakthrough comes from the parent doing their own work and developing enough capacity to distinguish between their activation and their child's.

When that happens—when a parent can look at their child's most difficult behavior and ask what this child's nervous system is trying to tell us instead of why this child is doing this to me—everything changes.

I think about Sidney—the one who came to me afraid her son was going to kill her. What happened in her healing was not just that she processed her own trauma. It was that processing her own trauma gave her eyes to see her son's.

She couldn't see him before because her own nervous system was too activated to look clearly.

Once she could look—once she could stay regulated in his hardest moments and bring genuine curiosity to what his behavior was communicating—he began, slowly and imperfectly, to feel seen. And a child who feels seen by their parent can begin to heal.

That is the ripple effect of parenting while healing.

We aren't striving for perfect parenting, just present parenting, regulated parenting—parenting that sees the individual child and asks, "What does this specific child, with this specific history, in this specific moment, actually need?"

That question—asked honestly, from a regulated nervous system—is the beginning of everything.

Your Journey

This journaling exercise is a space to notice what is shifting as you heal. There is no right way to parent perfectly. Only a way to become more present.

1. Noticing the Shift

As you move through your own healing, what are you noticing about how you show up as a parent (or caregiver)?

2. The Ripple

Where are you noticing changes in your child(ren) or in your parenting dynamic?

What feels different?

3. Learning From the Moment
Children often:

- feel
- notice
- express
- release
- and move on

What are you noticing about this in your child(ren) or in children around you?

4. My Activation
Are there moments when your child's emotions activate

something in you?

☐ Yes
☐ No
☐ Sometimes

If yes, what are you noticing in your body or reactions?

5. Gentleness

What would it look like to be gentle with yourself in these moments?

What would it look like to give your child time to adjust to your changes in parenting?

6. Presence Over Perfection

A moment where you showed up differently than you would have in the past:

7. Reflection

What feels important to remember as you parent while healing?

Closing Reminder

Parenting while healing is not about perfection. It's about presence. It's about noticing. It's about repairing when needed.

Take a breath. This ripple matters.

If you work with children or teens, rather than parent them – in a classroom, a therapy room, or a coaching relationship – this section is for you.

1. Noticing the Shift

As you move through your own healing, what are you noticing about how you show up with children?

2. The Ripple

Where are you noticing changes in your interactions with children (students, clients, groups, etc.)?

What feels different in your responses?

3. Understanding Children

Children often:

- feel
- notice
- express

- release
- and move on

What are you noticing about this in the children you work with?

4. My Activation

Are there moments when a child's behavior or emotions activate something in you?

☐ Yes
☐ No
☐ Sometimes

If yes, what do you notice in your body or reactions?

5. Regulation Before Response

In moments of activation, what helps you slow down or regulate before responding?

What might you want to try next time?

6. Shifting My Response

A moment where you responded differently than you might have in the past:

7. Gentleness

What would it look like to be gentle with yourself as you learn and adjust?

What might it look like to give children space to adjust to your parenting shifts?

8. Reflection

What feels important to remember as you work with children while healing?

Closing Reminder

Working with children while healing is not about getting it right. It's about being present, noticing, and responding with more awareness over time.

Take a breath. This ripple matters.

CHAPTER TWENTY-ONE

Boundaries Are Not Walls

The Story

I was seventeen years old, and I had a full scholarship to the University of Wyoming.

It was the practical, financially responsible choice, the choice that made sense on paper and that my father—with the particular certainty of a man who had strong opinions about money and practicality—believed I should make without further deliberation.

But I knew that I could not go there.

Not that I didn't want to. Not that it wasn't a good school. But something in my body—something operating well below the level of conscious thought—had already made its assessment. University of Wyoming was a large university with a large campus and a large student body in a large town. And I was a 17-year-old girl from a small Wyoming hometown whose nervous system had been calibrated to hypervigilance and whose relationship with safety was complicated in ways I couldn't have articulated at the time.

My body knew before my mind did. And what it knew was: this school is not safe enough for you.

My mother supported me. We spent several months touring colleges together—a season I remember as one of the first times I felt genuinely seen in a major decision, with my preferences mattering and my instincts being taken seriously. My father was upset and irritated. He and my mother found themselves on opposite sides of something that felt, to him, simple, and to me, essential. My parents pulled in different directions, and I stood in the middle, holding what I knew to be true.

I ended up at Rocky Mountain College in Billings, Montana, six hours from home. I was far enough away that I would have to build my own life but close enough that I could be home within a day's drive if something fell apart.

The campus was small—about the size of my high school. The student body was intimate. The setting was contained in a way that my nervous system could orient to, could map, could eventually trust.

I didn't have the language for any of this at 17. I didn't know I was protecting myself. I didn't know I was setting a boundary—not against a person, but against a situation that my body had already assessed as beyond its current capacity.

I just knew I wasn't going to the University of Wyoming. And I held that knowing against the friction it caused, even in the face of my father's irritation and against the financial logic that said I should be grateful and take what had been offered to me. I held fast against the discomfort I felt being the child who defied the expected path and cost someone something in the process.

I held fast because my body would not let me do otherwise.

That, I have come to understand, is what a real boundary feels like. Boundary setting does not always require a dramatic declaration or a confrontation. Sometimes you can set a boundary with a quiet, certain, immovable knowing on which your nervous system refuses to negotiate.

The Science

Imagine a field surrounded by a fence.

Inside the fence line are the things you protect, the values you hold, the experiences, people and spaces that belong in your life because they are nourishing or necessary or genuinely yours. And then there is what stays outside the fence—not because it is bad, necessarily, but because it does not belong on your field.

Boundaries are the fence.

Boundaries are not walls. Walls are different. Walls keep everything out—the harmful and the nourishing alike. Walls are built from fear and maintained by hypervigilance. They protect, yes, but at the cost of everything that requires openness to receive—intimacy, support, genuine connection.

A fence has a gate. It has a clear perimeter. It is tended consciously—you decide what comes in and what stays out, based on your own honest assessment of what belongs in your life and what doesn't. And crucially, the fence protects what is inside it.

Many of us grew up in homes where there was no fence, where a parent's emotional state became the child's responsibility, where privacy was not protected, where the child's "no" was not honored, and so the child learned that their "no" didn't matter. Or we grew up in homes where the fence was electrified—where rigid, punishing limits kept everyone at a distance and intimacy was never possible.

Neither background teaches a child what a healthy fence looks like or what it feels like to tend one, what it means to keep the gate closed when someone pushes against it.

Most of us arrive in adulthood without any fence-maintenance skills. We either have no fence—and we let in everything, exhaust ourselves managing the consequences, and wonder why we feel so depleted. Or we have a wall—and we keep everyone at a distance and wonder why we feel so alone.

Learning to build and tend the fence is the work of integration. It is, in many ways, the external expression of everything internal that this book has been asking you to do.

Here is something important that most conversations about limits miss entirely.

Your body knows where the fence should be before your mind does.

This is not a metaphor. This is the neuroscience of boundary-setting. The same sensory system that encodes threat and safety—that notices, before conscious awareness, when something is wrong—is the same system that registers when something is too much, too close, too costly, or simply not right. The body's assessment often comes well before the mind's understanding.

I didn't have the words to explain why the University of Wyoming was wrong for me at 17. But my body had already done the calculation. The fence line was already drawn. What I had to do was trust my instinct—hold my boundary against the friction it caused, honor the knowing even before I could explain it.

This is bottom-up boundary-setting. I didn't decide on a reasonable limit with my cortex, then try to enforce it. I listened to the body's honest assessment first—and then used my thinking brain to figure out how to honor what my body already knew.

Dr. Bruce Perry's Neurosequential Model helps us understand why this matters. The brainstem is always assessing. Always scanning. Always making rapid, below-consciousness calculations about safety and threat. When that system signals discomfort, contraction, the urge to move away or protect—that signal is information. It is not drama. It is not oversensitivity. It is the oldest and most reliable part of your nervous system, doing its job.

Learning to trust that signal—to honor it before you can explain it, to act on it even when others don't understand it—is one of the most important skills of integration.

Trusting your instincts connects directly to everything you've practiced in Part Four of this book. Just notice. Sit with it. Acknowledge it. And then—act from it. Build the fence where the body says the fence belongs.

At their most essential, limits are how the internal work shows up in the external world. They are the visible evidence of everything invisible that has shifted inside you.

The Skill: Boundaries

Building and tending the fence is a practice. It is not a single decision or a one-time declaration. It is an ongoing relationship with your own internal assessment.

Listen to your body first. Before you decide whether a limit is reasonable or warranted, notice what your body is doing. Where are you feeling a contraction? Where do you notice the impulse to move away, to protect, to say no before the mind has finished forming the thought? That impulse is information. Do not override it before you understand it.

Name what you are protecting. Every limit protects something—your energy, your safety, your healing, your values. When you can name what the fence is protecting, the fence becomes easier to hold—because you know what you're standing for.

Practice the small limits first. Say "no" to something low-stakes. State your preference when you'd usually defer. Set a boundary on something ordinary. These small practices build the muscle so that when a larger limit is required—when the stakes are higher, and the friction is greater—you have a practice to draw on.

Hold the fence through the friction. Limits almost always produce friction. People who benefited from your fence's absence will often push back the hardest. This is not evidence that your limits are wrong. It is evidence that they are real.

Repair when you can. Hold firm when you must. Not every friction point requires you to yield. Some limits are too rigid, too broad, set from fear rather than wisdom, and those deserve revisiting. But many do not. The discomfort of the person pushing against your fence is not your responsibility to resolve by removing the fence.

Know the difference between a fence and a wall. A fence has a gate. It is tended with intention—and allows you to consciously decide what comes in and what stays out, based on honest self-knowledge rather than blanket protection. If your limit is keeping out everything—nourishment and harm alike, intimacy and intrusion in equal measure—it may be a wall. And walls are worth examining with the same curiosity you've brought to everything else in this book.

From My Life

For most of my life, I was better at setting limits around safety than around ordinary life. I could leave a dangerous situation—that skill was well-practiced, hardwired into my nervous system from an early age. What I struggled with was the everyday fence. I had trouble saying no when saying yes felt obligatory or setting a limit with someone I loved without feeling like I was abandoning them. I did not know how to protect my own time and energy without guilt.

My college decision was one of the first times I held a limit that wasn't about survival in the obvious sense. Nobody was going to hurt me if I went to the University of Wyoming. But something essential—something my body understood before my mind did—would have been lost. I needed a sense of safety that I could manage at a place that was smaller. And I needed the physical distance from my family that would let me finally, at 17, begin to be someone separate from the family system I had grown up inside.

So I held that boundary—against my father's irritation and the financial logic.

And Rocky Mountain College gave me something I didn't know I needed until I had it: A small community, a campus I could walk across in 10 minutes and feel, eventually, that I belonged there.

That limit—set without full conscious understanding, held through friction—turned out to be one of the most important decisions of my life. Not because Rocky Mountain College was objectively better. But because my body knew what my nervous system needed—and I trusted myself.

I have spent my career watching people learn to trust that same knowing in themselves, watching clients discover that they already knew where their fence needed to be. Their bodies had been signaling them for years; the only thing missing was the permission to honor their own needs, their own boundaries.

You already know where your fence belongs. You have known for a long time. Your body has been telling you—in the contraction, in the exhaustion, in the recurring dread, in the relief when certain things end, and in the aliveness you feel when certain other things begin.

The fence is already drawn. Your work is simply learning to trust what you already know—and to hold firm when the friction comes.

Because the friction will come. But what you're protecting inside your fence line is worth it.

Your Journey

Boundaries are not something you force. They are something you begin to notice.

1. Body Signals
Something your body is saying "yes" to:

Something your body is saying "no" to:

2. The Fence
What feels inside your "fence" right now?

What feels outside of it?

3. Expression
What might it look like to honor one of these boundaries?

4. Practice
A small boundary you could practice this week:

Closing Reminder

Boundaries protect what is inside. They are allowed to change as you do.

CONCLUSION

The Emotional Spotter

There is footage taken from another ship in the Pacific on October 25, 1944. The YouTube video shows a Kamikaze pilot flying low over the water. The pilot hit the USS St. Lo.

My grandfather was on that ship.

His name was Grandpa Chuck. He survived—one of the few who did. He floated in the Pacific and watched his battle buddies die around him, and eventually he was pulled from the water and sent home to live the rest of his life with something that had no name yet. Shell shock. What we now call PTSD. An incomplete stress cycle of such magnitude that it reorganized everything it touched—his nervous system, his parenting, his capacity for connection, the particular quality of silence that lived in his house for the rest of his life.

He never spoke of it. He collected things instead. He sat in his Bronco for hours, sometimes days. He was always kind and always had a story to tell. But never that story. Never the one that explained everything.

A few years ago, I drove two hours across rural Colorado into rural Wyoming to sit at my father's table and ask to see Grandpa Chuck's military records. My daughter Stella came with me. We prepped for the visit the way you prep for complicated family territory—I told her what to expect, what subjects would and wouldn't come up, where the tender places were. We agreed on how long we would stay.

We had lunch. We visited about absolutely nothing. And then my father pulled up YouTube.

The three of us—my father, my daughter, and me—watched that 58-second video together. Watched the moment that had defined my grandfather's life. The beginning of a thread that ran through my father's childhood, through my childhood, through an ACE score of 7, through a divorce, through a deployment, through 20,000 one-on-one conversations, and this book.

After the end of that 58-second video, my father got up, walked to the refrigerator, pulled out a beer, and chugged it.

That was his off-ramp, the same one he had been taking his entire life. His stress cycle was running exactly as it always had—incomplete, unprocessed, seeking the familiar detour.

The dotted lines of generational trauma became solid lines in that moment. I could see them running from that ship in the Pacific through everything that had followed—through my grandfather's silence and violence, through my father's drinking and violence, through my own survival and healing and the specific work I was called to do.

And Stella—my daughter, the strong-spirited one, the one who practices “no” with the safest people on the planet—looked at me and said:

"Mom, I think it's about time we go home."

We drove two hours back across the Wyoming border into Colorado. And we talked about all of it. The surface-level lunch. The depth of those 58 seconds. The beer. The generational thread that had been running through our family for 80 years without anyone naming it, without anyone having the tools to complete what had started on that ship.

We talked about the dotted lines becoming solid lines and about how Grandpa Chuck survived without a spotter—and about how I spent my entire career becoming one.

I want to tell you about a Soldier.

He was 19 years old. I met him in the in-between places that military life creates—the hurry-up-and-wait, the days between planes, the margins of deployment where the real conversations happen.

I was in Iraq when we first met. He was passing through. We had time. And in that time—in a way that still strikes me as one of the gifts of this work—we unpacked some of his childhood history and did some Brainspotting together around a traumatic experience from when he was much younger. He responded well. I taught him how to use bilateral music on his own when he needed it. And then we both moved on to wherever the next plane was taking us.

About a month later, I landed in the UAE. He happened to be there. He asked to meet.

I said yes—because I always say yes to that ask. Because behind that ask is always something real and important.

We sat down. And he said:

"Ma'am, you know how when you go to the gym, and you're about to lift something heavy, and you ask someone to spot you? You still have to lift the heavy weight yourself, but someone is there spotting you. Well, that's you, ma'am. You're our emotional spotter. We still have to do the work and lift the emotional heavy weight, but you're there spotting us, helping us if it gets too heavy on our own."

I sat there after he went back to his barracks.

Stunned. Seen. Overwhelmed.

And I thought—I came all the way to the Middle East to meet with a nineteen-year-old Soldier so that he could give me the language of my life's work.

Thank you, God, for this moment.

That is what this book has been trying to give you—not a spotter who lifts the weight for you, not someone who bypasses the hard work or promises you won't have to feel it, but someone who stands beside you while you lift and knows the weight is real. You deserve a spotter who has felt their own version of that heavy lift and who will not look away when it gets heavy and will not pretend it is lighter than it is.

That is what good therapy offers. That is what good relationships offer. That is what this book has been trying to offer—page by page, chapter by chapter, story by story.

I have tried to be your emotional spotter through these pages.

But here is what I need you to understand before you close this book.

The spotting was always secondary. The lifting was always your job.

Everything in these pages—the stress cycle, the activation scale, the shape and color and size, the keeping and the releasing, the patterns that outlived the wounds, the relationships that healed and the ones that couldn't—none of it works without you doing the actual work. You have to be willing to notice, to sit with it, to acknowledge what is true, to let your body lead, to practice staying when the pattern says leave, to repair when you miss, to keep showing up for the relationships worth keeping and to release the ones that are no longer safe to hold.

That is not a small ask. I know it isn't. I have done it myself. I am still doing it—in every season of my life, with every new layer that surfaces, with every moment where the Trainwreck of the Unconscious™ reveals something I didn't know was still running.

Healing is not a destination. It is a practice. It is the willingness to keep returning—to your body, to your awareness, to the tools you now have—every time the rubber band stretches and needs to release.

You are more capable of this than you know.

I have watched people do this work in therapy rooms, training rooms, hospital waiting rooms, and military bases in the Middle East. I have watched people who were certain they could not survive what they were carrying not only survive it, but eventually integrate it, file it, and let it become part of their story without becoming the whole story.

I have watched people's activation shift from a 10 to a seven... from a seven to a four...from a four to something manageable, neutralized and no longer running the show.

I have watched the rubber band release.

And I have thought about my grandfather every time.

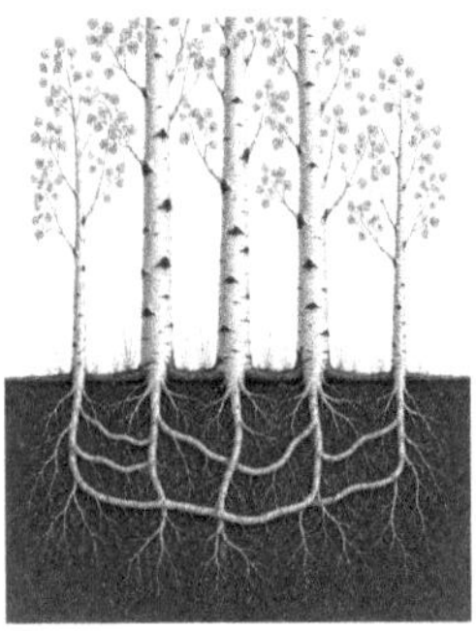

I think often about aspen trees.

You know what I know about them by now—the rhizome root system, the clonal colony, the single organism that appears to be a forest of separate trees. Individual trunks live and die while the root system beneath them persists for thousands of years, continuously sending up new growth as older trunks age and decline. The Pando clone in Utah—one of the largest and oldest living organisms on Earth—is a single aspen that has been growing from the same root system for thousands of years.

What looks like separation is connection. What appears individual is shared. Life above the ground is temporary. The roots underneath are ancient and persistent.

My grandfather's unprocessed trauma was a root. It sent up trunks—in my father, in my father's parenting, in my childhood, in the ACE score I carried into adulthood. Those trunks were shaped by what the root held. Some of them grew in ways that caused harm. Some of them survived. Some of them—this one, in particular—grew toward healing.

Breaking a generational cycle does not sever the tree from

the roots. The healing tree grows differently from the same root system. May you be the trunk that chooses a new direction—not because the roots are gone, but because you finally understand what the roots have been carrying. You now have the tools to grow toward something different.

Grandpa Chuck survived the USS St. Lo. He came home without a spotter. Without anyone who could stand beside him and say, "I see what you are carrying. I will not take it from you. But I will stand here while you lift it."

That absence rippled forward for 80 years.

And somewhere in the middle of a deployment, in the in-between places of a military base, a young Soldier sat across from that traumatized man's granddaughter and gave her the language she had been living her whole life without knowing.

The roots sent up new growth.

And the new growth—you, reading this—are part of the same living thing.

You have done something significant in these pages.

You mapped your story. You built your safety. You practiced the skills. You sat with the hard things, let some of them release, and chose to handle others differently. You looked at the patterns that outlived the wounds and began—imperfectly, courageously, one 30-second turn-around at a time—to practice something new.

You can't unknow what you know.

And the knowing—however disorienting, however costly, however much it changes the shape of your relationships and your life—is a gift. This has always been available in the space between stimulus and response. That is the space where freedom lives. Where choice becomes possible. Where the trunk can finally grow in a direction toward which the roots have never reached before.

Trust your brain. Trust your body. Your body will lead.

And when it gets heavy—and it will get heavy, because this

is real work and real weight—remember that you are not alone in it.

You never were.

The emotional spotter is beside you. Not lifting for you. Never lifting for you.

Just here. Present. Watching you do something extraordinary.

You've got this.

Now go live your life. Come back to these pages when you need them. They will be here.

And so will I.

A NOTE ON GOING DEEPER

Dear brave reader,

I'll be honest. The course came first. Then the book.

I don't believe anyone should heal alone and without a relationship. So I developed an online course—videos that walk you through everything in this book, in my voice, at your pace. I built a community where people who took the course could share their wins, support each other, and emotionally spot one another—with me as a guide.

And then I realized, more people will read the book than can take the course. Books can reach people that courses can't. They find their way into the hands of people who weren't looking for them, who pick them up in airports, gift them to friends, and leave them on nightstands for years.

So now that you've read this book, I want you to know that there is more, if you want it.

I invite you to the online community. This is the place where the course lives—videos of me telling these stories, walking you through these skills, sitting with you in the work the way I have been sitting with you in these pages. It is a place where you will meet others who are healing. Who are going through similar things. Who will understand what you mean when you talk about the rubber band, and the lava, and the Trainwreck of the Unconscious™, and the end of the block.

Our online community is a place where you don't have to explain yourself from the beginning.

A place where you don't have to heal alone.

You've done something brave in reading this book. If you're ready for the next thing—whatever that is, whenever that is—I'm here.

Come find us.

Scan this QR code to learn more about the Becoming an Emotional Spotter course.

BIBLIOGRAPHY AND RESOURCES

Books

Frankl, Viktor E. *Man's Search for Meaning*. Beacon Press, 1959.

Gibson, Lindsay C. *Adult Children of Emotionally Immature Parents: How to Heal from Distant, Rejecting, or Self-Involved Parents*. New Harbinger Publications, 2015.

Gomez, Ana M. EMDR *Therapy and Adjunct Approaches with Children: Complex Trauma, Attachment, and Dissociation*. Springer Publishing, 2012.

Maté, Gabor. *The Myth of Normal: Trauma, Illness, and Healing in a Toxic Culture*. Avery, 2022.

Ogden, Pat, Kekuni Minton, and Clare Pain. *Trauma and the Body: A Sensorimotor Approach to Psychotherapy*. W. W. Norton & Company, 2006.

Perry, Bruce D., and Maia Szalavitz. *The Boy Who Was Raised as a Dog: And Other Stories from a Child Psychiatrist's Notebook*. Basic Books, 2006.

Siegel, Daniel J. *The Developing Mind: How Relationships and the Brain Interact to Shape Who We Are*. Guilford Press, 1999.

Further Reading

Brummer, Joe, Margaret Thorsborne, and Lori Desautels. *Becoming a Trauma-Informed Restorative Educator: Practical Skills to Change Culture and Behavior*. Jessica Kingsley Publishers, 2023.

Gobbel, Robyn. *Raising Kids with Big, Baffling Behaviors:*

Brain-Body-Sensory Strategies That Really Work. Jessica Kingsley Publishers, 2023.

Healy, Ginger. 15-*Minute Focus: Regulation and Co-Regulation: Accessible Neuroscience and Connection Strategies that Bring Calm into the Classroom*. National Center for Youth Issues, 2022.

Perry, Bruce D., and Oprah Winfrey. *What Happened to You?: Conversations on Trauma, Resilience, and Healing*. Flatiron Books, 2021.

Post, Bryan. *From Fear to Love: Parenting Difficult Adopted Children*. Post Institutes and Associates, 2010.

Apps for Regulation and Support

Calm—guided meditation, sleep, and bilateral music

Bondify.ai—AI-powered, trauma-informed parenting platform that offers real-time personalized guidance for parents, especially adoptive parents

Insight Timer—free meditation library and community

Headspace—guided mindfulness and stress reduction

Resources

SAMHSA National Helpline: 1-800-662-4357 (free, confidential, 24/7)

988 Suicide and Crisis Lifeline: call or text 988

www.ingramcontent.com/pod-product-compliance
Lightning Source LLC
LaVergne TN
LVHW050909210926
848482LV00012B/383
9798996117604